Praise for
In the House of Memory

"Steve Rabey opens a door to a once-forgotten
spiritual heritage that has special relevance today."
—Edward C. Sellner,
author of *Wisdom of the Celtic Saints*

"Rabey retells the stories of monks and monasteries,
and celebrates the Celtic affection for silence,
solitude, and prayer, and the Celtic love for learning
in a manner that is irresistible."
—*Publishers Weekly*

STEVE RABEY's articles have appeared in *The New York
Times*, *The Washington Post*, the *Los Angeles Times*,
Christianity Today, and *New Age*. He is the coauthor,
with John Michael Talbot, of *The Lessons of Saint
Francis*, also available in a Plume edition. He lives in
Colorado.

Also by Steve Rabey

The Lessons of Saint Francis

IN THE HOUSE OF MEMORY

Ancient Celtic Wisdom for Everyday Life

STEVE RABEY

A PLUME BOOK

PLUME
Published by the Penguin Group
Penguin Putnam Inc., 375 Hudson Street, New York, New York 10014, U.S.A.
Penguin Books Ltd, 27 Wrights Lane, London W8 5TZ, England
Penguin Books Australia Ltd, Ringwood, Victoria, Australia
Penguin Books Canada Ltd, 10 Alcorn Avenue, Toronto, Ontario, Canada M4V 3B2
Penguin Books (N.Z.) Ltd, 182–190 Wairau Road, Auckland 10, New Zealand

Penguin Books Ltd, Registered Offices: Harmondsworth, Middlesex, England

Published by Plume, a member of Penguin Putnam Inc.
Previously published in a Dutton edition.

First Plume Printing, November, 1999
10 9 8 7 6 5 4 3 2 1

 REGISTERED TRADEMARK—MARCA REGISTRADA

The Library of Congress has catalogued the Dutton edition as follows:
Rabey, Steve.
    In the house of memory : ancient Celtic wisdom for everyday life / Steve Rabey.
        p.   cm.
    Includes bibliographical references and index.
    ISBN 0-525-94409-5
            0-452-27953-4 (pbk.)
1. Spirituality—Celtic Church. 2. Celts—Ireland—Religion. 3. Spirituality—Ireland.
4. Celtic Church—Doctrines. I. Title.
BR748.R33   1998
299'.16—dc21   98-8116
                                                                                CIP

Printed in the United States of America
Set in Galliard
Original hardcover design by Leonard Telesca

Contents

Give more thought to my subject than to my words which I consider rough and of little worth.

—St. Columba

INTRODUCTION:
A DISTANT SPLENDOR

*I am reading about Celtic monasticism, the hermits,
the lyric poets, the pilgrims. . . . A whole new world
that has waited until now to open up for me.*

—Thomas Merton

THE RECENT PERFORMANCE SPECTACLES *Riverdance* and
Lord of the Dance have probably done more to popularize some aspects of Celtic culture than anything else this
century, but they haven't been alone in exposing people to
the beauty of this ancient world. Best-selling books like
Angela's Ashes and *How the Irish Saved Civilization* and the
haunting music of recording artists Enya and the Chieftains
have served as sirens, beckoning the curious to explore the
Celtic world. "My God!" said Nobel Prize–winning Irish
poet Seamus Heaney. "Ireland is chic!"

Unfortunately, this modern revival has provided us with
only a partial knowledge of Celtic culture, and we may
sense a gap between our enthusiasm and our understanding. We can't fully grasp from them the deeper meaning of
many Celtic traditions, and as a result, we're oblivious to

their continuing worldwide influence. What's worse, we're cut off from the deep wisdom and abiding comfort some of these traditions have to share. It is out of a desire to see that gap closed a bit that this book was born.

Who were the Celts?

Long before the Romans ruled, it was the Celts who had conquered much of the known world. Emerging in the millennia before the Christian era, they came from Asia and Russia, where they shared common linguistic and cultural roots with other ancient Indo-European peoples. By around 390 B.C., the Celts' fierce fighting men and women had even advanced on Rome itself. Aristotle wrote that Celtic warriors feared nothing and fought naked. With their powerful metal swords and battle-axes (and it was the Celts, not Vikings, who wore helmets decorated with big horns), and their terrible war cries, these ferocious warriors soon controlled much of Europe from the Mediterranean to Scandinavia and established major outposts in Gaul and Brittany.

The Celtic peoples migrated to the British isles around 500 B.C., where they quickly subdued the native tribes. By the first century A.D., the Romans had over-taken major Celtic strongholds in Europe and southern England, but the Romans never conquered the Celtic outposts in Wales and Scotland, and they never even attempted invading Ireland, a land that was seen as too remote and strategically insignificant to be worth the effort. As a result, it is in these areas of the Celtic fringe—Ireland, Wales, Cornwall, and Scotland—that one can still find the strongest elements of Celtic culture today.

The Romans portrayed the Celts as primitive barbarians who fought by day and feasted all night. When St. Paul wrote his letter to the Christians in Galatia around A.D. 50, he urged believers in this pagan Celtic stronghold to avoid idolatry, sorcery, hatred, and murder. But the Celts also possessed a flair for art and design, exhibited a love of language and literature, and, as we'll see, were a deeply spiritual people who constructed elaborate tombs to house the dead and developed extensive rituals to honor the many deities they worshipped.

Much of our information about the Celts comes from archaeologists, who have unearthed impressive metal jewelry, cauldrons, and other implements, uncovered massive graves, and found traces of ancient farms and fields. Not until the fifth century, about the time St. Patrick migrated from Britain to Ireland to preach and accelerate the process of Christianization that had already begun, are there written records of the Celtic past. But if there is much we will never know about the history of the Celts, Ireland today remains a storehouse of ancient Celtic lore. "Ireland is the only country in Western Europe that still has contact with its archaic origins," writes author Andrew Greeley.

▣ A living spiritual tradition

The complex history of Ireland and the British Isles is only a part of the broader Celtic story, and much of that bigger story is about spirituality. In fact, the Celtic people may have had a greater hunger for the divine than just about any people the world has ever known. "A capacity for worship," writes Celtic scholar Anne Ross, "a passionate feeling for the supernatural, for the gods, or, later, God, is, I believe, the truest and most binding cultural element throughout the entire Celtic world."

Whether they were building lasting monuments to hundreds of pagan deities in prehistoric times, or retreating to island monasteries during the sixth and seventh centuries so they could meditate on the glories of the Christian creator God, the Celtic people seemed always to be intent on putting spiritual principles and practices first and foremost in their daily lives.

Thankfully, the Celtic areas of England, Scotland, Wales, and particularly Ireland, remain rich storehouses of Celtic spiritual wisdom and lore. In addition to the ancient monuments and buildings which dot the landscape, the present-day people who trace their ancestry back to the ancient Celts possess powerful memories of centuries-old legends, traditions and myths, many of which are intimately connected with the land itself. Thus the people and the land represent houses of Celtic memory, and even first-time visitors are often amazed by how this rich, communal memory can reach out and touch them today.

That vibrant spiritual memory remains attractive to people across the religious spectrum. Some are drawn to an ancient and exotic pagan spirituality that, even if vaguely understood, remains highly evocative. Others are moved by the earth-centeredness of Celtic Christianity. For pagan Celts, the physical world was full of otherworldly deities and spirits, and ritual was meant to acknowledge that reality. For Christian Celts, the natural world bore the signature of God, and nature was the best chapel in creation.

Still others find comfort in the Celts' gender inclusiveness and egalitarianism. Both men and women fought in battles, served as druids and druidesses, and were ordained as priests and spiritual directors. Celtic society, both pagan and Christian, allowed women to exercise their plentiful gifts, and that radical approach had a transforming effect on Celtic spirituality as well.

And who doesn't admire the Celts' creativity, their ingenuity, their literary achievements, and their moving music? For Celtic people, spirituality didn't result in a retreat from the world and a diminished view of the physicality of life on earth. Quite the contrary. Nearness to the divine brought forth a spiritually enhanced urge to create, from the pagan Celts who gave us some of the wildest and woolliest legends of ancient times to the Celtic Christians who believed they had been made in the image of an all-powerful God. In the pages that follow, I hope to trace the threads of Celtic spirituality from its pagan origins to the intermingling of ancient traditions with the Christian faith, seeking out ways that we can affirm these enduring principles in our own lives today.

According to his biographer, the Celtic St. Ciaran of Saigir "lived in this life, poor in worldly matters, rich in divine matters." The same could be said for the Celts in Ireland. Theirs was an island so remote and inconsequential that the empire-building Romans virtually ignored it, and modern Ireland has continued to struggle with poverty and deprivation. Ireland and its Celtic neighbors have hoarded a spiritual wealth, however, that still gleams in its distant splendor and draws the curious and hungry as it did centuries ago. It is to that wealth that we now turn.

1

LOVE OF THE LAND

Divinity is imminent in all Nature. It is as much within you as without.

—Margot Adler, *Drawing Down the Moon*

RURAL IRELAND IN THE 1930s is the setting for John Keane's disturbing drama *The Field*. For forty years, Bull McCabe worked a small, rented patch of earth, growing vegetables and grains for his small family and his animals, much as his father had done for forty years before. He nourished the soil with dung from his animals and with seaweed, which he laboriously carried on his back over hills and through valleys from the ocean, more than a mile away.

Over the course of his life, that small field became as big a part of McCabe's life as his wife and son and their tiny, humble cottage. Visiting the small plot was an essential part of the rhythm of life. It was a rare day when McCabe didn't check on his plot, tend to his crops, or till fresh seaweed into the rich, fertile soil. "I know every rib of grass and every thistle and every whitethorn bush that bounds it," says McCabe.

When the widow who owned the field put it up for sale, McCabe was too poor to buy it himself and watched in horror as his beloved plot was purchased at auction by an ambitious American who planned to develop the land and, even worse, cover it over with concrete. "It's ag'in God an' man," says McCabe, as he watched his life and his livelihood disappear before his eyes.

The Field is much more than an examination of one man's deep connection to a small parcel of land. Rather, it's a glimpse into an entire culture's devotion to the soil on which their ancestors lived and died. This devotion moved ancient Celtic people to turn the raw materials of earth and stone into majestic monuments designed to help them commune with the invisible forces they believed to lie within nature. Centuries later, hundreds of Christian monks and mystics fled to the most remote and desolate spots of Ireland's rugged wilderness where they could be unencumbered in their worship of a God they lovingly called "the Lord of the Elements." More recently, the spirit of the land inspired the poet Gerard Manley Hopkins to write "The world is charged with the grandeur of God." Even today, there's a wild beauty to Ireland that surprises seasoned travelers who think they've seen beauty before. What's more, many say, they sense a spiritual presence in the land.

🔲 Pagan pantheists

Mention the words *pagan* and *heathen*, and people who don't consider themselves to be either may exhibit a hostile reaction that, when one does a little probing, turns out to be heavy on negative connotation and light on real understanding. The suspicion surrounding the terms is largely a consequence of centuries of conflict that intensified when followers of the Christian faith gave up trying to persuade those who worshipped other gods to follow their God, and instead began trying to convert them with guns and government acts.

The term *pagan* comes from the Latin words *pagus*, which urbane city dwellers used to describe an uncultivated rural area, and *paganus*, which they used to describe a person who lived in such a wild region. Similarly, "heathen" originally referred to a person who lived in the heaths, or open wastelands full of wild shrubs, including heather.

But when people use the word *pagan* today, they're not talking about a rustic country bumpkin, but rather a believer in strange things, a practitioner of odd rituals, or an adherent of an older, simpler, earth-based, nature faith that twentieth-century neo-pagan Margot Adler calls "radical pantheism."

The ancient Celtic people, who lived outside the circumference of both written history and organized religion, didn't think of themselves as pagans. They probably didn't even think of themselves as particularly religious. Rather, theirs was a primitive people's spontaneous expression of a sense that the world and everything in it, including themselves, was sacred. Or as Adler puts it, "The world is holy. Nature is holy. The body is holy. Sexuality is holy. The mind is holy. The imagination is holy. You are holy."

Without written records, it's impossible to spell out precisely what the early Celts believed. But that's where archaeology helps us. Working in Ireland, Scotland, Wales, and parts of Europe, and digging through tons of accumulated earth, rock, and debris, researchers have uncovered statues, sculptures, and other depictions of an estimated four hundred distinct Celtic deities. Among the more widely known gods and goddesses was Danu, a mother goddess for whom the Danube River is named. The Celts once lived along the banks of the Danube, which flows through present-day central Europe to the Black Sea. Another pagan deity known to many Celts was Lugh, a warrior god identified with weapons, crafts, and the victory of the sun over darkness.

But deities like Danu and Lugh are unusual, for what archaeologists find most interesting is that more than three hundred of the Celtic deities they have so far identified appear only once. Most of these deities were local, and many were connected to a specific geographic feature, such as a mountain or a stream. As a result, they were probably worshipped by only a small group of people, family, or tribe. The existence of so many localized deities shows us that the Celts believed that the earth on which they lived and depended was sacred, and that each force of nature, and possibly even each feature of the landscape, partook of divinity.

The Spirit of the Place

Everywhere the Celts went, they left their cultural imprint on the land. Today, we can see this legacy best through the names they left on the landscape. From London, which the

Celts called "the fortress of Lugh" after one of their pagan deities; to the Danube River, originally named after the Celtic goddess Danu; to Paris, which was named after the Parisii, a migrating Celtic group, their impact reaches far and wide.

In Europe and the British Isles, there are more than a thousand place-names that begin with the letters *ra*, *rah*, *raw*, *ray*, or *rath*. The origin of these names is simple. The Celts called their ring forts made out of earth and rocks *rath*. Over the centuries, many of these simple forts evolved into towns and cities, but they have maintained a tie to their humble, ancient origins.

Many place-names are tied to Celtic spiritual practices. Red Hill, located near Skreen, Ireland, was formerly called Knocknadrooa, which means "hill of the druids." More than sixty Irish place-names begin with some variation of the word *knock*, which is Irish for "hill," including Knockatober ("the hill of the well") and Knockaderry ("the hill of the oak wood").

Armagh, a city long connected with St. Patrick and for centuries claimed to be Ireland's foremost Christian site, was originally named after a pagan goddess, Ard-Macha.

Another popular Irish prefix is *kil*, meaning church. Many place-names beginning with the *kil* prefix are named after churches dedicated to particular saints or holy men and women,

such as Kilbeggan ("Beccan's church") or
Kilcolman ("St. Colman's church"). Others
reflect the church's environment, such as
Kilcullen ("church of the holly") or Kilfithmone
("the church of the wood of the bog"). There
are more than fifty places named Kilmurry, or
"church of the Virgin Mary."

And a little village on the Welsh island of
Anglesey claims the world's second longest
place-name: Llanfairpwllgwyngyllgogerych-
wyrndrobwllllantysiliogogogoch. It means
"Church of Mary near the white-hazelnut
spring near the wild maelstrom by the
Sysitis-chapel in the red cave."

🔲 Natural cathedrals

Ruth Bidgood, a twentieth-century Welsh poet, is
one of the latest in a centuries-long line of writers to be
inspired by something the Welsh call *hud*, a sense of
wonder and awe at the presence of divinity in nature.
She frequently writes about standing stones, church ruins, and the smallest natural details in and around her
beloved Cambrian Mountains. Her poem "Hoofprints"
is a marvelous example of the Celtic love for the natural
world, relating the legend that a set of hoofprints carved
in a local rock were created by a magic horse who
pranced among the hills on the day the valley was born.
While questioning the absolute truth of the legend, Bidgood recognizes its attempt to come to grips with the

majestic forces of nature. "From the unseeable, legends leap," she writes.

From legend, too, comes the name of one of the most impressive landmarks in County Kerry. You can see the twin peaks from miles away, glimpsing them from the road that runs from Ballyvourney to Glenflesk. Locals call them "the Paps," and indeed the huge mounds resemble women's breasts. Their full name, in Irish, is *An Da Chich Danann*, or in English, the Paps of Anu. To ancient Celts, who deified the earth as their mother, the peaks were thought to represent the breasts of the earth-goddess Anu, the source of fertility and fruitfulness whose presence is remembered throughout the Celtic landscape in such place-names as the Scottish town of Annan.

The Paps, as well as numerous other hilltops and high places, were seen as sacred sites that were inhabited by gods and goddesses. Over the course of centuries, the human presence on these hilltops mirrored the transitions in Celtic society. At first, the hills were the sites of elaborate nature rituals. In time, they hosted large, seasonal tribal gatherings, then heavily fortified town settlements. The valleys of rivers like the Danube and the Boyne were revered as domains of the goddess. It was believed that shorelines—those places where water and land met—were sacred junctions where people could receive spiritual insight as well as poetic inspiration.

The Boyne Valley

Perhaps no place in Ireland played so full a part in the development of the Celtic tradition as the Boyne Valley. Like many other places in the Celtic landscape, the Boyne is named after a pagan deity, the goddess Boann. The Boyne begins at Edenderry, a town about thirty miles west of Dublin on the east coast of Ireland. From there, the river snakes northward and eastward until it empties into the Irish Sea at Drogheda, about twenty-five miles north of Dublin. The Boyne Valley was one of the first places humans settled after they arrived in Ireland, and the history of the place reads like chapters from the book of an ancient people.

Newgrange, which overlooks the Boyne near the town of Slane, bears the oldest evidence of humans' presence on the landscape. It is also one of the earliest and most magnificent burial chambers in the world, older than both the Egyptian pyramids and Stonehenge. About ten miles west of Newgrange lies the Hill of Tara, thought to be the most sacred place in Ireland for centuries. Long the Seat of Ireland's High King, the hill was also an important pagan ritual site crowned by earthen circles. About fifteen miles north lies the Hill of Slane, associated with the Christian tradition, and these two hills played a dueling role in the loyalties of the Celtic people.

About fifteen miles northwest of Tara is the town of Kells, which grew up around the monastery founded by St. Columba. The town is synonymous with Christian learning and art through its association with the Book of Kells, one of the most prized illuminated manuscripts in the world. Kells, along with Monasterboice, a monastery north of Drogheda, was also famous for its beautiful Celtic crosses. These stone monuments are a lasting symbol of Celtic Christianity, which reinterpreted the faith in new ways and transported it to a Europe that was then entering some of its darkest days just as the Celts were experiencing a cultural explosion.

About midway between Newgrange and Drogheda the River Boyne heads due north before turning and heading east again. Here in 1690, the Protestant William, Prince of Orange and later William III of England, defeated the forces of the Catholic King James II, the last Stuart monarch. This decisive Battle of the Boyne was to be the beginning of the end of Irish independence, marking a waning of Celtic influence in the valley where it had seen its fullest expression.

If hills and rivers were believed to be the haunts of female deities, forests and groves were seen as areas where male deities frolicked. Sacred groves full of sturdy oaks with broad branches created a kind of natural cathedral, whose dense foliage gave both seclusion and intimacy to those who gathered there. As we will see, the druids were said to have officiated at rituals in the groves, and the word *druid* originally meant "oak knower." The ancient Celts also revered rowan and hazel groves as sacred sites.

Unfortunately, no druid composed a firsthand account of the rituals that went on in the groves. Instead we have reports from Romans and Greeks, most of whom didn't try to conceal their contempt for the Celts of Gaul. Lucan, who wrote in the first century A.D., was horrified at the "barbarous rites" and "a sinister mode of worship" conducted by druids in "deep groves" and "solitary places":

> A grove there was, untouched by men's hands from ancient times, whose interlacing boughs enclosed a space of darkness and cold shade, and banished the sunshine from above. . . . Gods were worshiped there with savage rites, the altars were heaped with hideous offerings, and every tree was sprinkled with human gore. On these boughs . . . birds feared to perch; in those coverts wild beasts would not lie down; no wind ever bore down upon that wood. . . .

The Roman historians objected to the connection of these groves not only with scenes of human sacrifice, but also with sexual activity. The Celts inhabited a physical world that they believed to be surrounded by otherworldly gods and goddesses, many of whom coupled with abandon. The Celts viewed sexuality as a sacrament, and many ancient fertility festivals were accompanied by abundant copulation. During their coronation celebrations, some Irish kings had sex with horses, symbolizing the relationship earthly rulers were believed to have with nature's fertility. To the participants, these practices may have been sacred, but to the Roman conquerors and Christian evangelists, it all looked distinctly profane. Debates over whether such practices elevate or debase sexuality will undoubtedly continue.

❈ Sacred stones

The discovery of the wheel some five thousand years ago is hailed as a watershed event in the story of human development. A parallel development in the story of human spiritual development is the use of the ritual circle, something our pre-Celtic ancestors were beginning to practice even earlier. The pagan Celts created and abandoned thousands of stone circles, many of which stand as silent reminders of mysterious ancient rites.

One never forgets the first glimpse of a circle of upright stones, rising from the flat ground like silent sentries. The strangeness of their appearance, combined with the mystery surrounding their construction and original intent, provokes the kind of profound feeling writer F. Scott Peck expressed in his memoir, *In Search of Stones*. During a visit to England in his youth, he saw a row of standing stones from a fast-moving train and felt the desire to stop the train and embrace them. "The sight has haunted me ever since," he writes. "It has stayed so vividly in my memory I'd even wondered whether it might not have been a dream."

Today, there are hundreds of remaining installations of standing stones and stone circles one can visit throughout Europe and the British Isles. At Almendras in Portugal, ninety-five standing stones make up a pair of oval-shaped circles. At Carnac, near the coast of Brittany, France, three thousand stones—the largest grouping of upright stones in Europe—are laid out in a series of straight rows.

But the most famous of all megalithic sites is England's Stonehenge. This massive monument evolved over a period of fourteen centuries until four thousand years ago, when it took its present form, consisting of thirty large upright stones topped by lintel stones. Building Stonehenge would have required sophisticated engineering and massive communal planning and execution. One engineer has estimated that it would have taken a team of fifteen hundred men two months to transport each one of the thirty upright stones twenty-four miles across the local countryside.

A nearby complex of earth and stone would have been even more impressive than the celebrated Stonehenge was in its day. Avebury, which covers some twenty-eight acres, was home to what was probably the largest stone circle in the world. Surrounded by a huge, circular earthen berm, Avebury's main stone circle consisted of ninety boulders each weighing five tons, along with two smaller circles of thirty stones each. And just south of this massive complex, man-made Silbury Hill rises nearly two hundred feet from the southeastern English plains. Contemporary researchers estimate it would have required some eighteen million man hours to build the hill, which consists of some twelve million cubic feet of hand-carried chalk and other material.

The beautiful Preseli Mountains of Wales are believed to be the source of many of the huge bluestones used at Stonehenge, but the mountains' own Gors Fawr stone circle consists of sixteen stones that are much smaller in scale—most under two feet tall—making it more typical of most of the hundreds of stone circles that dot the Celtic lands. From the Merry Maidens circle near Penzance in Cornwall, to the taller stone slabs that make up the Callanish standing stones on the Isle of Lewis, these ritual circles were silent witnesses to the spiritual practices of the ancient Celts. We probably will never know all we would like to about when these monuments of stone and earth were built or by whom or for what. But like F. Scott Peck, we remain awed and mystified by them.

❧ Love of nature, love of God

By the time Christian evangelists arrived in Ireland in the fifth century, most of the Celts' impressive monuments were no longer in use. Many of them fell into disrepair, were covered over by brush or bog, or were raided and used for building materials. Some were used as the cornerstones for churches of the new faith. But while the monuments crumbled, love of the land beneath them remained an essential part of the Celtic consciousness.

The Celtic Christians kept that love alive, even though they did so for radically different reasons from their pagan predecessors. Unlike the pantheistic Celts, who saw divinity everywhere, the Celtic Christians were monotheists who saw divinity in God alone. But that doesn't mean they dismissed the natural world as irrelevant or unimportant. Instead, they saw nature as sacred. However, that sacredness was not due to any inherent divinity, but derived from the fact that nature had been fashioned by God, whom St. Patrick called "the Creator of all Creation."

St. Patrick recorded his beliefs in an ancient document known as a "breastplate" or "lorica," a traditional Celtic form of prayer that was shared by pagan and Christian alike. (These breastplates were believed to protect the person who recited them, conveying supernatural powers.) Though Patrick's breastplate is clearly Christian, complete with references to the Trinity, Christ's crucifixion and resurrection, and the Patriarchs and Prophets of the Church, many of its verses wouldn't have sounded strange coming from the lips of a druid chanting in a sacred grove:

> I arise today
> through the strength of Heaven:
> light of Sun,
> brilliance of Moon,
> splendor of Fire,
> speed of Lightning,
> swiftness of Wind,
> depth of Sea,
> stability of Earth,
> firmness of Rock.

It's difficult picturing Christians in Rome reciting such a rapturous song to the natural world. In fact, for most of Christian history, leading Christian thinkers have held a much less appreciative view of nature. Some theologians saw the natural world as fatally flawed by the Fall of Adam and Eve, while others viewed this life as a vale of tears to be patiently endured while awaiting the eternal, heavenly home. Sadly, it was this more negative view that became widespread in later centuries, leading many twentieth-century environmentalists to implicate Christianity in the widespread destruction of the environment. They argued that the Christian view stripped nature of its divinity, thus paving the way for exploiting and abusing it.

Patrick and his Celtic brothers and sisters would have been repelled by such a negative view of God's creation. Until his death in 1946, British scholar Robin Flowers, spent a good portion of his time researching the lives and beliefs of the people of Ireland's remote western isles. Flowers concluded from his study that Celtic Christians looked at nature with "an eye washed miraculously clear by continuous spiritual exercises," and as a result, they had a "strange vision of natural things in an almost unnatural purity." In the words of storyteller Peig Sayers, one of the modern mystics Flowers encountered, "There is a freshness and brightness in everything God created."

🪢 Natural saints

Following in the footsteps of Patrick, an immigrant to Ireland who had been raised in a Romano-British setting, came hundreds of Irish-born monks who had inhaled the Celtic love of the land as surely as they had inhaled their fair isle's fresh, brisk air. Chief among them, St. Kevin, founder of the famous monastery located in the beautiful valley site of Glendalough, sought to return to the innocence of the Garden of Eden, and in the process he created a popular movement of nature-loving monks. As with other Irish saints, it's hard to separate the fact from the fantasy in Kevin's biography, but all accounts reveal his deep reverence for all that God created.

One legend relates that Kevin had befriended an otter. Once, the animal allegedly retrieved his Psalter from the lake—a recurring episode in the lives of saints who happened to live near water and were dedicated students. After that, the same otter regularly delivered fresh salmon to Kevin and his brothers. Another time, Kevin commanded a wolf who had killed a doe's fawn to spend the rest of his life as the doe's surrogate child.

On another occasion, Kevin was out in the wilderness, fasting and praying to God in solitude, a common practice for Irish monks. As Kevin prayed, a cow approached and licked the saint's feet. That night, the cow produced as much milk as half of the rest of the herd. Day after day, the cow licked Kevin's feet, and night after night it produced an abundance of milk. The herdsman determined to follow the cow, so he could see what pasture she was eating in and take the rest of his cows there. But instead he found Kevin, who was weak and feeble because of his fasting. After much protesting from Kevin, the herdsman carried the saint through the woods to a spot God had chosen for his church. And all along the way, the trees of the forest bent their trunks to give the herdsman room, making it easier for him to carry Kevin to the appointed site.

Like Kevin, St. Cuthbert, who is best known as an abbot of the famous monastery of Lindisfarne off the eastern coast of Scotland, had a closeness with otters. Cuthbert would frequently spend the late hours of the night up to his neck in frigid water praying, a practice that was adopted by many of the ascetic-minded Celtic saints. But Cuthbert had a comfort other monks didn't: After his prayers, two otters would warm his feet with their breath and dry him with their fur.

In the lives of many of the Celtic saints, one finds numerous examples showing how the saint's intimacy with God led to intimacy with God's creatures. Legend has it that St. Ciaran, founder of the important monastic center of Clonmacnoise, counted among his closest companions a badger, a doe, a wolf, and a wild boar who became his first monk. A fox was said to carry the saint's Psalter, but only when a stag wasn't lending his horns to be used as a natural bookstand. St. Gobhnat of Ballyvourney, one of Ireland's female saints, had many animal helpers, including nine white deer, who showed her where to build her monastery, and a flurry of buzzing bees, who guarded the site from intruders.

As a boy, Ailbe of Emly narrowly escaped a king's death sentence when a slave hid him under a rock. The wild wolf who lived under the rock came to love the boy, and "fondly nourished him among her own cubs." And once when St. Columbanus was reciting a psalm, twelve wolves approached him and stood meekly as he recited God's word. He also reportedly conversed with squirrels. Columbanus founded many Celtic monasteries throughout Europe, including one in the Italian town of Bobbio, which was visited by another nature-loving saint, the young Francis of Assisi, centuries later.

Among the many saints whose lives reveal a closeness with nature, St. Columba, one of the most beloved Celtic saints, is an especially important figure. Columba may have been a pagan before he converted to Christianity. His lingering adherence for the old ways can be seen in the layout of the monasteries he founded at Derry, Durrow, and Kells, each of which bordered an oak grove. At Doire, he prohibited any trees to be cut while his monastery was being built. But on the subject of his most famous monastery at Iona, founded on an island off the western coast of Scotland, Columba gives fullest expression to his feeling for nature:

> Delightful I think it to be in the bosom of an isle
> on the crest of a rock,
> that I may see often
> the calm of the sea.
>
> That I may see its heavy waves
> over the glittering ocean
> as they chant a melody to their Father
> on their eternal course.

Columba's heartfelt connection to the Celtic world's centuries-old love for the land, his clear-eyed vision of the relationship between creation and the Creator, and his predilection for writing poetry about the beauty he saw all around him made him an inspiration to many nature writers who would follow after him.

▨ Courting creation

The main reason so many people don't appreciate nature today is that they haven't done anything to strike up a relationship. But by following the example of the Celts, we can learn how to care for creation as they did.

- **Take a nature walk.** Our ancient Celtic ancestors would be shocked at how little contact many moderns have with the natural world. In *The Field*, Bull Mc-Cabe died soon after he learned he would be cut off from his beloved plot of land, and in many ways, we die a little bit from living lives that are hermetically sealed off from the wildness and the wonder of nature. Some of us are barely surviving in conditions so nearly fatal that the only prescription is an emergency immersion in the nearest park, zoo, forest, or shore. Once you get there, you can sit, walk, stand, run, or dance, but under no condition should you take books, beepers, cell phones, or portable CD players. Instead, give your weary senses a brief respite from the incessant din of human culture by letting them luxuriate in the feel of the wind in your hair, the sight of a squirrel on a nearby branch, the smell of freshly cut grass or fallen leaves, the sound of birds singing their beautiful little songs, and, if you have the opportunity, the taste of the salt in a sea breeze. Don't try to analyze what you're feeling. Just enjoy the experience of letting creation sing around you.
- **Care for a plant.** Contrary to popular opinion, no one is incapable of nurturing a houseplant. One of the proofs of the bounty of nature is that there are many

flowers and plants that will suit your house, your budget, your personality, and your skill level. Some require less work than microwaving an instant dinner. Ask for help at your local plant store. Usually, all you need is a little space, a window or a lamp for light, and a little water. That's a small price to pay for bringing the beauty of creation into your home.

- **Plant a garden.** If you're ready to move into more serious contact with nature, plant a garden, a tree, or a bush. There's nothing like crawling around on your hands and knees and sinking your hands into the soil to give you an immediate and powerful sense of connection with the natural world. There are plenty of books and magazines around that can help you assess what will grow where in your yard. Or, many garden stores will provide a free consultation. Once you have established your bit of Eden, set aside a certain time of day when you can sit quietly and reflect upon creation in your garden. And follow the changing seasons, observing the natural rhythms of nature that can instruct and comfort us.

- **Teach kids to appreciate the natural world.** Next time you're looking for something fun to do with a child or grandchild, skip the mall and head for a park, the zoo, or an arboretum. Help members of the younger generations—many of whom have even less contact with nature than you do—to marvel at creation. Perhaps you can join a wildlife or conservation organization together and learn more about preserving habitats and endangered plants and animals by participating in their activities together.

- **Take poetry to the park.** If you're not sure why people make such a big deal about the beauty of nature, buy a collection of nature poetry, or even a copy of Thoreau's *Walden*, and take it to the nearest park. As you read, look around you, connecting the wonders you see to the ones you're reading about.

- **Be earth-friendly.** There are a million ways to walk softly on the earth. One is to be careful about the products you buy. Stay away from things that contain or are manufactured using hazardous materials. Watch the chemicals you use on your lawn, and consider pulling weeds instead of poisoning them. And if you invest in the stock market, consider making investments in firms that don't pollute.

- **Put down your own roots.** The ancient Celts identified deeply with the land where they were born. But today, many people have come to believe that relocating and leaving one's birthplace, one's parents, and one's friends represents progress. We leave home to go pursue our education, to get a better job, to secure a promotion within the company, regardless of the sadness we may feel about pulling up our roots. Despite the career gains, there is something permanently lost along the way—relationships with friends, as well as a more intangible sense of community, that sense of knowing where you're from that was so important to the Celts. Before you make that next move, take time to reevaluate your priorities, remembering the value of place and friends and family.

2

The Bonds of Kin and Clan

When an Irish person asks "Who are you?" the question really means, "Of what people do you spring?"

They call it Dunbeg Fort, or Dun Beag in Irish, which was the language that was spoken when it was built some twenty-five hundred years ago. Although it may appear today as a meaningless heap of rock and rubble, Dunbeg was in earlier times an important refuge for a number of Celtic tribes, providing safety and protection to a series of ancient clans. Strategically located on a finger of land that was virtually unreachable by sea, Dunbeg was safe in its splendid isolation. Over the past twenty-five centuries, erosion has claimed much of the land that surrounded the house and, today, the rocky fortress is just a few feet away from the perilous cliffs overlooking Dingle Bay. But in its day, one could have walked around the house without any fear of falling into the sea.

Throughout Ireland's rough and rugged landscape, there are remnants of thirty to forty thousand forts, most of which were built by Iron Age Celtic people between 500 B.C. and A.D. 500. But in addition to being among the most numerous and widely distributed reminders of a people and a way of life that has now mostly vanished, these many forts are also a powerful symbol of one of the strongest links uniting Celtic society—the bonds of kin and clan.

We're not sure who built Dunbeg, or who they were hiding from, but whoever constructed this massive project knew how to thwart a foe. Dunbeg is a maze of mounds, ditches, ramparts, tunnels, and trap doors that would have repelled all but the bravest or stupidest of attackers. The focal point of the whole site is the clochaun, or beehive house, which was built in the traditional dry-stone manner, without mortar. Instead, the walls of the house, which are many feet thick, depend on gravity to hold them together.

The landward side of the house didn't have the sea to protect it, so its residents constructed a massive stone wall that cuts across the finger of land like a big, gaudy bracelet. Built of carefully stacked stone, the rampart is over twenty feet high and nearly ten feet thick, and it extends across the promontory for nearly one hundred feet. A survey taken in the 1850s records that the wall was then twice that long—an indication of the toll erosion has taken over the last century and a half. The side of the rampart facing the house is stair-stepped, so family members could climb up and position themselves to defend their home. In addition, the one passageway through the wall, which is a low and narrow affair, is guarded on either side by hidden chambers, from which a defender could plunge a spear or shoot an arrow at unwanted intruders.

Outside the rampart, the tiny peninsula widens and here the family settlement is protected by a complex series of embankments. Five rows of ditches, called fosses, range from three to five feet deep and are between twenty and forty feet wide. Between the five rows of fosses are four rows of banks, which are approximately three feet high and ten feet wide. These banks and fosses wouldn't have prevented determined marauders from getting close to the stone ramparts, but they would have slowed the invaders down, making them vulnerable to attack from defenders of the fort.

Excavations of the site have turned up some tantalizing information. For example, we know the house was inhabited as early as 580 B.C., and as late as the tenth or eleventh century A.D. Holes in the earth indicate that inhabitants once erected tripod stands out of trees, from which they hung cooking pots over large fires. Throughout the house area are remnants from meals of sheep, pigs, and fish. There's also evidence of an underground hiding chamber, or souterrain, where residents could hide belongings—or themselves—if their defenses were breached. In addition, there are flagstone walkways, as well as a brilliantly designed drainage system, which would have kept the seaside settlement as dry as possible.

🔲 Rock solid sites

Dunbeg isn't the biggest or even the most impressive Iron Age Celtic fort. For sheer breathtaking beauty, one turns to Inishmore, the largest of the Aran Islands off Ireland's western coast. There sits Dun Aengus, the most impressive and best known of all Ireland's stone forts. One scholar has called it "the most magnificent barbaric monument in Europe."

Like Dunbeg, Dun Aengus is protected on its back side by the sea. And what a protective barrier these ancient Celts had. The fort's central court abuts a sheer rock cliff two hundred feet above the Atlantic, seemingly vulnerable only to a hero from the pages of Celtic mythology. On the fort's landward side, a series of four stone walls radiate outward in ever-widening D-shaped half-circles. Each ring of walls protects a small area of land, with the innermost wall being the most massive—twelve feet high and twelve feet thick. Outside the walls is a series of small, upright stones. Unlike other standing stones, which have a clear ritual role, these were purely defensive, and were designed to slow the progress of an approaching attacker.

Despite intense research by an international chorus of scholars, as in the case of Dunbeg, no one knows who built Dun Aengus, when, or why. Nonetheless, wherever the Iron Age Celts went, they built massive forts, adapting their architecture to the lay of the land and the local conditions. Certainly, one of the most unusual ancient forts is Doon Fort, which was constructed on a small island in Doon Lough, County Donegal. The massive stone walls rise fifteen feet, outside of which there are a few yards of land leading to the edge of a surrounding lake. The fort occupies around ninety percent of the island land mass. Again, nothing is known about the fort's builders or history.

An interesting variation on these rocky forts is the hillfort, which was built atop inclines and seems to have served both practical and spiritual needs. About fifty known examples of the hillfort survive in Ireland. Although they differed in their styles, all the Celtic forts had a common role: to give safety and shelter to family members while keeping intruders at bay.

🪡 Celtic family ties

As we have seen, the Celts felt a deep connection to the land. Now it is clear that a major component of this strong sense of place was related to the deep bonds of blood, kin, and clan. Ancestry and geography are so thoroughly intertwined that when an Irish person, speaking the Irish language asks, "Who are you?", the question really means, "Of what people do you spring?" This deep sense of connection to a place that has been passed down from generation to generation is a difficult thing for many moderns to grasp.

Perhaps an even greater challenge for people in our culture, where individualism is highly valued, if not enshrined, is to comprehend how the Celts understood the individual only in the context of his or her connections to larger familial and social groups. The Celts would have failed to understand our willingness to suffer the consequences of our lifestyle choices, including personal loneliness and alienation and skyrocketing rates of divorce and family breakdown. The Celts didn't have a concept for self-fulfillment, but if they had, they would have believed that such happiness could come only through commitments to family and kin.

Historians speak of the Celtic hereditary tradition. We often think of inheritance in terms of receiving the deceased's worldly possessions. In Celtic culture, one inherited much more than possessions from ancestors. One also received from the family one's name, much of one's identity, and most of one's role in the larger society. In fact, up until a thousand years ago, individuals in Ireland didn't own land; families did.

The Celts also had a deep respect and, in many cases, reverence for their ancestors. At times such respect resembled ancestor worship, making the Celts seem a lot more like the traditional Japanese than like their Western neighbors. Most Celts even believed their ancient ancestors were gods. In their view, the world was created by these legendary ancestors. And on a smaller scale, the world most Celts inhabited on a daily basis—which included a hut or stone house, with a small area for crops and animals, and often was connected to other such dwellings—was seen as a gift of ancestors both recent and ancient.

The influence of these ancestors didn't end with their deaths. Instead, they were believed to continue looking after the living, helping to insure their prosperity and success.

▣ Clan and tribe

The basic building block of Celtic society was the clan, a group of people sharing common ancestors and a common name who were organized under the rule of a chief. Larger and more complex than the now-standard nuclear family of father, mother, and children, the clan was an extended family or kinship group often called *derbfhine*, which was Irish for "certain family." Usually, the clan consisted of descendants in the male line going back to a common grandfather, so one's clan would include one's second cousins.

The next building block of Celtic society was the tribe, which was a very extended family, including all who considered themselves to be of a common ancestry. Over time these tribes, which could include hundreds or thousands of people, were subsumed into a system of petty chiefdoms. And by the time Christian evangelists started arriving in Ireland in the fifth century, the system of chiefdoms was giving way to a system of larger royal states, each of which was controlled by a king who controlled many lesser chiefs.

None of this wrenching social transition was accomplished peacefully, so perhaps we can begin to see why a tribe would build a Dunbeg or a Dun Aengus, and why they would have surrounded their tribal area with so many walls, hills, and ditches. The typical Celtic clan lived through cycles of calm and chaos. A family could enjoy years of relative peace, during which they could concentrate on raising their children and their crops. But then warfare would break out between two clans, two tribes, or two kingdoms, and families would have to be prepared for a series of raids on their homes, their family members, and their livestock.

Perhaps it's no surprise that Celts covered the land with forts during the Iron Age, a time in which life could often be incredibly nasty, brutish, and short.

▦ The Celts' sacred kings

If all you know about Celtic kings are stories of the legendary King Arthur, you're in for a surprise. For one thing, Arthur—who, if he has any basis in fact whatsoever, came from the Celtic area of Wales—is portrayed as the ruler of a sizable kingdom, the high king over a number of loyal knights. But in reality, it's doubtful any Iron Age Celtic kingdoms were as vast or as centralized as some of the Arthurian legends seem to imply.

For example, by the time of St. Patrick, Ireland had many petty kings and kingdoms, or *tuatha*. Some scholars say there were as few as eighty Irish kings at any one time. Some say there may have been hundreds, each ruling over anywhere from five hundred to twelve hundred souls in a country with a total population estimated to be around half a million people.

What we do know is that each king engaged in a variety of pacts and conflicts with the others. When things were working well, each petty king would have owed allegiance to one of a half dozen or so provincial kings, each of whom would owe ultimate allegiance to a ruler hailed as the High King. Both the title and the location of the High King's seat changed often. The most legendary Irish High Kings ruled from Tara in the Boyne

River Valley, near Newgrange. But even though Celtic myths and legends talk about the great deeds of the High Kings, it's doubtful that they really wielded as much power and control as the bards they employed said.

On the other hand, the Arthurian legends did get one thing dead right. Celtic kings were viewed as semisacred beings, and the good ones were believed to be important intermediaries between this world and the otherworld. Much of the material in the legends gives Arthur a decidedly Christian character, probably the result of repeated retellings during later generations, when there was more of a Christian influence. But earlier Celtic kings were decidedly pagan in their orientation and ritual roles. As Celtic scholar Liam de Paor puts it in his book *Saint Patrick's World*, the king served as a kind of communal guardian, providing both physical and spiritual care "to protect a pastoral and agricultural people against the arbitrary forces of nature, such as drought, storm, famine, lightning and disease, imagined as malevolent interventions by divinities or otherworld beings."

Further, the king was seen as more than the ruler of his people; he was the mate of the goddess of the area. At times, this partnership between the earthly king and the otherworldly goddess was acknowledged in a variety of symbolic celebrations and rituals. At other times, the rituals were made surprisingly real. De Paor describes how, during the elaborate inauguration ceremony for the king of Cenel Conaill, one of the northern provinces, "at an assembly of the people a white mare was brought to the chosen man, who mated publicly with the animal, which was then killed, cut up, and boiled. All ate the mare's flesh and the new king bathed in the broth and drank it." According to de Paor, prehistoric kingship "was intimately connected with pagan religious belief."

One can imagine how St. Patrick and other Christian monks would have looked upon these rituals. They viewed this behavior as a mix of superstition and bestiality. But to the Celts, such rituals were viewed as an essential glue holding their society together. Over time, many Celtic kings would convert to the Christian faith, but others remained firmly committed to their pagan beliefs and practices.

❖ The sacred and the sensual

In *Angela's Ashes*, his Pulitzer Prize–winning 1996 memoir about growing up in the slums of a wet and grimy Limerick, Frank McCourt peppers his account of his "miserable Irish Catholic childhood" with stories about extreme sexual prudishness. In one memorable passage, McCourt describes a Redemptorist priest scolding young male students about sexual sins that cause the Virgin Mary to turn her face away in anguish. "She weeps when she looks down the long dreary vista of time and beholds in horror the spectacle of Limerick boys defiling themselves, polluting themselves, interfering with themselves, abusing themselves, soiling their young bodies, which are the temples of the Holy Ghost," he writes.

In another passage, McCourt describes a hilarious episode that happened when he was sixteen and worked for a Limerick magazine distributor. After helping make sure dozens of shops had their copies of *John O'London's Weekly*, McCourt was ordered to hop on his bike, revisit all the shops, grab copies of the periodical, and rip out a condom ad that appeared in the journal. "Now go for God's sake and bring back every page sixteen you tear out so that we can burn them here in the fire," screamed his boss.

This type of Victorian moralism about sexual matters represents a dramatic swing away from the ancient Celts' easygoing approach to sex. Perhaps nowhere is this more dramatically seen than at Killinaboy, a tiny church in western Ireland's County Clare, which is decorated with a most unecclesiastical-looking sculpture. Over one of the doors is carved an ancient image of a female goddess called a Sheela-na-gig. Her large crude face is smiling. Her body is relatively small and simplistic. But her hands reach between her legs and part her grossly oversized vulva in a gesture that seems both an invitation to sex and a reminder of the goddess's fertility.

The Sheela-na-gig, a popular idol that appeared repeatedly throughout Celtic lands, is a symbol of the pervasiveness of sexuality in those societies. There was such a thing as marriage, and of course there was sex between men and women who were married, but all such marriages were renewable on an annual basis, and many couples opted for other mates when the year expired. Furthermore, many other men and women formed partnerships and coupled without even the flimsiest of contracts or commitments.

Sex was also a part of many of the regular festivals celebrated throughout much of the Celtic world. Ancient Celtic communities depended on the bounty of their crops and the fertility of the earth. Since it was believed that the earth and humans were spiritually linked, it made perfect sense for these regular fertility festivals to be marked by the liberal coupling of the communities' able and healthy members. It was also common, well into the nineteenth century, for couples to make love in the fields surrounding a house where a corpse lay. According to Andrew Greeley, the custom was a way for pre-Christian Celts to say, "Screw you, Death. Life is stronger than you!"

Unlike traditional Western faiths, where there is a solid theological line between the holy and the human, and especially between the holy and the sensual, for the Celts the two were linked. "There is no trace of a Celtic goddess of love," writes Celtic scholar Anne Ross, "but all the goddesses share in having marked sexual characteristics, and no matter what their individual departments of influence, sexuality and maternity are their fundamental concerns."

One of ancient Ireland's most important epics, the *"Tain Bo Cuailnge"* or "The Cattle Raid of Cooley," features gods and goddesses scheming and cavorting against a backdrop of rural concerns and simmering sexuality. In one memorable scene, Queen Medb plots to acquire a prized bull. Barking out orders to Mac Roth, the chief messenger, she tells him to acquire the bull for a year in exchange for fifty yearling heifers and other inducements, including "a fine portion of the fine Plain of Ai equal to his own lands, and a chariot with thrice seven bondmaids, and my own friendly thighs on top of that."

Perhaps it's no surprise, then, that while the Celts were deeply committed to kin and clan, they also engaged in polyandry, polygamy, and communal marriage;

and what marriages there were were highly unstable, with divorce and remarriage being common. The Venerable Bede records that the Roman Catholic hierarchy struggled to bring Britain's formerly pagan Celts into harmony with the teaching and practice of the church. When a bishop who is sent to the isles to oversee the harmonizing asks Pope Gregory, "To what degree may the faithful marry with their kindred?" the pope replies, "Since there are many among the English who, while they were still heathen, are said to have contracted these unlawful marriages, when they accept the Faith they are to be instructed that this is a grave offense and that they must abstain from it."

▧ The social web

It's easy to look back at the Celts' complex social, political, and sexual entanglements and declare the whole unnecessarily messy. But from the perspective of the average ancient Celt, this messy network was a vital safety net. These people lived in a state of near-perpetual concern about the uncertainties of nature and even a constant state of fear of attack from neighboring tribes. There's security in numbers, and the average Celt was surrounded by dozens, possibly hundreds, of kinsmen and friends. Psychological problems like alienation or anomie were virtually unknown in a society where everyone knew his or her place—physically, biologically, and spiritually. As Celtic scholar Nora Chadwick notes, "This tie of the 'kindred' was the strongest of all their early institutions."

In addition, individual kingdoms would often establish relationships with others in a complex system of fosterage, which enabled children of one kingdom to be raised and trained by the adults of another. The fosterage system allowed children to learn from others, helped adults forge strong ties across political lines, and even helped nurture an early welfare system, which ensured that virtually no one would wind up alone and without support.

Perhaps it's not surprising that the early Christian evangelists, whose own tradition extolled the family of God and spiritual brotherhood, emphasized those elements when they proclaimed the Gospel message. And their support for these important Celtic institutions was more than skin-deep. Many early Celtic saints were products of or supporters of the fosterage system. For example, both Brendan and Findbarr were fostered by elders in the faith, and both Ita and Maedoc fostered others.

But beyond that, these Celtic saints established an extensive monastic system that in many ways mirrored the extended family of the Celtic tribe. As numerous monastic "cities" became the primary social centers of their day, these monasteries became known for their hospitality, providing housing, food, and work for many people who had nowhere else to go, and making care for the poor a high priority. Writing of St. Aidan, a Celtic monk whose compassion was well known, the Venerable Bede comments that "if the wealthy ever gave him gifts of money, he either distributed it for the needs of the poor . . . or else he used it to ransom any who had unjustly been sold as slaves." And it is said that Guaire, a holy man who was never recognized by the Irish as a saint, was a powerful role model of compassion who "gave alms till his right arm grew to be longer than the left, with the dint of stretching it out to the poor."

Monks and monarchs

In addition to caring for people at the low end of society's totem pole, the early Celtic saints also learned how to connect with those at the top. According to the early saints' biographies, the monks' habit of mixing with Celtic kings resulted in goodwill, opened doors for spiritual conversion, and led to generous bequests of land and resources.

According to "The Life of St. Ailbe," the monk who built his monastery at Emly—near the important Celtic kingdom of Cashel—was adept at the art of dealing with kings. This near contemporary of St. Patrick asked King Aengus to grant the largest Aran island to his brother, the abbot St. Enda. The king replied he had "neither seen nor heard of any such island." At that point, a divine power enabled Aengus to see the island in the distance, and having seen it, he granted it to Enda, who founded an important monastery there.

Legend also tells us that Ailbe allegedly raised three sons of King Fintan from the dead. Of course, he did so after making the king this intriguing offer: "If you will believe and accept baptism, I will ask for divine help for you and for your sons." The king was converted and the sons were raised, at which point Ailbe made another promise: "Because you have believed in Christ you will overcome your enemies." So, Fintan went to war against the king of Connachta, "and had his revenge on them."

Not all of the dealings between the Celtic monks and the monarchy ended so well. In 607 at the Battle of Chester, hundreds of monks from the Dunawd monastery in Wales ascended a hill above a battlefield, where they prayed for British soldiers to defeat the invading Anglo-Saxons. When the Anglian forces won the battle, they ascended the hill and butchered the monks.

As the fortunes of various kings rose and fell like the waves of the sea, the wiser monks learned to avoid entanglement in the ephemera of worldly politics. And the limited, regional nature of most Irish kingships meant that these early efforts in church-state collaboration were much more humble than the later Holy Roman Empire. But in many instances, the Celtic saints continued to have an influence among the Celtic chiefs and kings, thereby winning new converts to their faith.

Family troubles

Using the building block of the extended family, the Celts created strong clans, powerful tribes, and large kingdoms. They were able to construct a strong and vibrant culture, aspects of which are still with us today. But just as every family suffers its share of storms and conflict, the Celts' commitment to a family-based society brought its own problems. Some of those problems had to do with the early Celts' inability to build an empire, and are now a part of ancient history. Others remain with us in the form of clannishness that divides Northern Ireland from the Republic of Ireland and Catholic from Protestant.

Flash back to 500 B.C. The Celts are rapidly expanding throughout Europe. Their sturdy metal swords are frightening enemies into flight. Their skill at agriculture is bringing them comfort and abundance. Their mastery of various arts and crafts is yielding some of the most impressive pieces of art in all of ancient history. The world was theirs for the taking—but they didn't take it.

Historians have puzzled over the fact that the once-dominant Celts were soon forced into the fringes of Europe, from where they sailed to the British Isles, where they were again, before long, forced to the fringes of Wales, Scotland, and remote Ireland. Why didn't they make a bid for empire? Why did they cease to be a dominant cultural power and instead allow themselves to be the subjects of other rulers?

The best answer that anyone can come up with is that the Celts had no real interest in empire building or the bureaucracy that sustaining such an empire requires. As John O'Riordain points out, the Celts were a simple agrarian people, whose closeness to the land and their own family roots yielded a localized emphasis rather than a quest for empire. "Their primary interest seems to have been human relations and living in the here and now," writes Irish-Catholic priest O'Riordain. As a result, we'll never know what kind of empire the Celts could have created. Instead, empires were built by the Romans and others.

Now, flash forward to 1969, and the beginning of a period that Irelanders remorsefully refer to as "the Troubles." Ever since 1690, when Protestant William of Orange defeated Catholic James II at the Battle of the Boyne, Ireland has witnessed all manner of Catholic-Protestant conflicts. During much of the eighteenth and nineteenth centuries,

Protestant English ruling powers subjected Irish Catholics to brutal suppression. But "the Troubles" represented a new phase of the conflict, as members of the renegade Irish Republican Army began using systematic violence to achieve their goals. Since that time, more than three thousand people have been killed in the sectarian violence, and thousands more have been injured.

Time after time, appeals have come forward for reconciliation and negotiations; but time after time, such appeals have been drowned out by the noise of further violence. While many still hold out hope of peace, other skeptics blame the ancient Celtic tribalism—a value that helps build strong local communities but that can become parochial and proud, preventing the construction of a peaceful larger society, or a modern democracy. Certainly, centuries of conflict with the British have let loose many demons, but many wonder if some of the demons now troubling Ireland don't spring, at least in part, from the overemphasis on the narrow bonds of kin and clan.

▣ Applying the best of the Celtic commitment to kin and clan

Even though Celtic tribalism has caused its share of problems, there's also much to be admired in how the Celts and their descendants have honored the bonds of family and heritage. Here are a few ways to apply these values in your own life.

- **Honor your family of origin.** Whether you search ancient Celtic myths and legends, or the Ten Commandments, the wisdom of the ages indicates that it's a mistake to neglect one's forebears. The Celts took respect for ancestors to bold new heights, worshipping an elaborate canopy of ancestor gods that looked over the living and promised them abundance and fertility. But many people today seem to have taken respect for parents to new lows. What would respect for family mean now? For some, it might require little more than seeking out regular contact with parents or relatives, checking in on them, and listening to them. In other cases it might mean giving up a job-related move to stay put and care for an ailing loved one. In any case, it means seeing yourself as part of a larger familial whole.

- **Build your own family.** No matter what kind of family you inherited, you can create a strong family of your own. Building a family requires time, attention, and love. Today, many couples are cutting back on work to spend more time with children. This may mean that neither of you create any empires, but you will be putting your family on a strong foundation.

- **Preserve your family history.** Celtic myth and history are full of the great deeds of the High Kings and various ancient families. But who tells the tales of your own family's history and deeds? Perhaps you can create a newsletter for your family, featuring current news and century-old history, illustrated with photos of everyone from new children to great-great-grandparents. Videotape interviews with family elders, in which they tell about family traditions and the good old days. Seek out ways to capture and retell your family history instead of letting it disappear.

3

DRUIDS AND HEROES

*Many of us have been drawn to Druidry because of
its evocative power.*

——Twentieth-century "druid" Philip Carr-Gomm

VINCENZO BELLINI SET HIS popular nineteenth-century opera *Norma* against a backdrop of the culture
of the pagan Celts. The opera opens in a large clearing in
the middle of a wooded area in Roman-occupied Gaul.
It's the night of a new moon, around 50 B.C. As your
eyes adjust to the darkness, you can see figures gathered
in the murky gloom. They're circling a large, solitary oak
tree that rises majestically in the clearing, and at the base
of the oak you can just barely make out an upright stone,
four to five feet high, which appears to be the focus of
attention for the dozens gathered in the glade. Then,
without any warning, one of the figures sings out:

> O druids, go up in to the hill
> and look out into the skies
> for when the silver crescent
> of the new moon is revealed;

and let three strokes
of the priests' mystical gong
announce the first smile
from her virginal face.

Next, as if on cue, dozens of figures start singing in unison, chanting out a song of anticipation for the powerful druidess, and for the next two hours these figures continue darting in and out of the clearing.

There's just one problem. Nearly every brushstroke in Bellini's elaborate portrait of the druids is little more than a wild fantasy stretched over the thinnest basis of fact. But don't blame Bellini. Instead, blame William Stukeley, an English physician turned Anglican priest turned homegrown antiquarian, whose love affair with Stonehenge and overheated imagination led him to create a whole body of elaborate lore that influenced generations of British history buffs.

Born in 1698, Stukeley began making a series of annual pilgrimages to Stonehenge in the early 1700s. Unimpeded by either the limits of the truth or a sense of academic humility, he created an intricate picture of druids worshipping serpents at Stonehenge, a picture that had such lasting appeal that the druid-Stonehenge connection remains powerful to this day.

Even before Stukeley's time, druids made frequent appearances in popular Irish myths and legends, such as the *"Tain Bo Cuailhge."* They may have been the inspiration for the cauldron-stirring witches in Shakespeare's *Macbeth*, the tale of a High King of Scotland that has had an important role in forming people's impressions of early pagan spirituality. In the 1800s, scores of bedazzled Brits tore down their gazebos and replaced them with hand-constructed, Stonehenge-like druid "temples."

And in the twentieth century, druids have come to life in a series of popular revivals. One such revival swept England earlier this century and saw a young Winston Churchill hosting a ceremony at his family's famous Blenheim Palace, during which he was installed into the Albion Lodge of the Ancient Order of Druids. And today, various quasi-religious groups claim they are the ancient druids' spiritual descendants. But like Bellini's *Norma*, many of these popular conceptions of druidism are light on fact and heavy on fantasy.

In reality, the druids were a complex group who seem to have held important spiritual, social, and political roles in Celtic societies throughout Europe and the British Isles. As with other prehistoric subjects we've explored, there's much we'll never know for sure about this mysterious bunch. And in the case of the druids, the historical vacuum is in part self-imposed: they cautioned against writing anything down, favoring instead the use of memory.

🕸 In search of the druids

Understanding who the druids really were requires a little preparation. First we have to remove the hazy misinformation that has clouded our understanding of this dynamic and important group. Perhaps the best way for us to approach the druids is to compare their plight to that of the Native Americans. Both sprang from ancient oral cultures that left no written records. That opens the door to self-appointed interpreters who say they've un-covered the truth about the groups' beliefs and rituals. Accounts of these belief systems are often short on docu-mentation and long on the use of words like *mysterious* and *magical*.

In addition, both groups were invaded by outsiders—outsiders who were convinced that they were ethnically, culturally, and spiritually superior to the people they had conquered. Anthropologists can debate the relative mer-its of conflicting cultures forever, but one thing's clear: When two cultures clash, it's the victor who writes about the vanquished. Often such written records are woefully incomplete and tragically tone-deaf to the nuances and subtleties of the conquered group. Sometimes, the vic-tors' reports aren't even designed to be truthful, and in-stead are written for propaganda purposes, justifying the violence used by the "civilized" to contain or punish the "heathen." In the case of the druids, we don't have a single piece of documentary material written by a sym-pathetic contemporary observer. Instead, everything we have comes from invading Romans and evangelizing Christians. Both groups were critical of the druids' pa-gan leanings, and often they could hardly disguise their contempt for some of the druids' practices.

Further, both druids and Native Americans have been hijacked by the New Age movement. Ever since the 1960s, there's been a scramble to uncover and exploit old, esoteric belief systems. Unfortunately, in the process of dredging for ancient truths, many New Agers mangle the very material they claim to be honoring. As Philip Carr-Gomm, Chief of the Order of Bards, Ovates, and Druids, writes in his 1996 book, *The Druid Renaissance*, "Many of us have been drawn to Druidry because of its evocative power—it conjures up images of wise sages, of ancient wisdom, and secret lore." Others, usually the more academic, have avoided Druidry because of the dearth of substantiated facts about its history, and the plethora of fantastical speculation it has evoked over the centuries.

🔹 Sacred and secular roles

If we really want to understand who the druids were, another comparison can help us out. As Peter Berresford Ellis does in his definitive study, *The Druids*, we can compare these ancient figures to India's Hindu Brahmins. It's a juxtaposition that makes good sense, plus it takes into account the fact that the Celts originally sprang from the same Indo-European cultural roots as India's Hindus.

Both druids and Brahmins assumed a variety of important roles in their respective societies. First, there were cultural roles. Druids and Brahmins formed the intellectual elite of their ancient worlds, and included among their numbers members of various learned professions, including philosophers, judges, teachers, and astronomers. Second, both druids and Brahmins played various political roles, with some serving as politicians, others as political advisors, and still others as professionals employed by rulers.

And third, druids and Brahmins both performed a variety of complex and sometimes confusing spiritual tasks. They presided at various ceremonies, just as priests or rabbis now preside at large state funerals. They also acted out important ritual duties and conducted whatever large public religious gatherings there were in their day. They also probably served more private and informal roles, working with Celtic chiefs and kings, giving spiritual advice to rulers, interpreting natural events like the weather or strange displays in the skies, and helping to legitimize the Celtic view of kings as semisacred beings. In the case of the druids, there are good arguments to be made that they also functioned as seers, sages, and shamans. In these roles, the druids would have worked as hands-on holy men, serving as vital conduits between the world of humans and the magical worlds just beyond the normal senses.

Today, there are a few common mistakes people make in trying to understand the druids. One is to concentrate solely on their religious and spiritual roles, ignoring the important "secular" power and influence they wielded. The second is to inflate the spiritual responsibilities with utter disregard to the few facts we do know about them.

Perhaps Ellis states it most clearly when he describes the druids as "an indigenous Celtic intelligentsia." Such a view helps to put the druids in proper context without limiting their importance. For as one scholar said, the druids were "the most enlightened and civilizing influence in prehistoric Europe."

🔲 In the company of kings

Without the Celtic kings, there may not have been the druids. During the centuries in which the Celts spread throughout much of the known world, their culture became increasingly complex. First, the Celts began by organizing themselves into numerous small, local clans that were sometimes little more than enlarged extended families. Next they evolved a system of larger tribes, and then a system consisting of numerous local chiefs and kings. These kings were not only rulers and warriors, but they were also believed to be earthly representatives of the gods.

Each king had a retinue of advisors, assistants, and hangers-on. The size of the retinue varied according to the power, wealth, and allure of the king. But any king worth his ale employed at least one tale spinner. The ancient equivalent of the modern official's public affairs officer or spin doctor, the tale spinner's main job was to herald the praises of the king. If a warrior king had been victorious in battle, it would have been easy for the druid to compose a few stanzas of verse that gave a blow-by-blow report of the brilliant defeat of the enemy. But if the king lost a battle, or killed his queen, or made a drunken fool out of himself at a big banquet, the situation called for the highest levels of skill and creative storytelling.

One of the most interesting and controversial areas in Celtic research involves ascertaining the roles of druids and bards. When we try our hardest to peer back into the ancient Celts' history, there's confusion about the relationships between these two important figures. It's clear that both were considered an essential part of a king's retinue, and both were considered a part of the same elite social class. But did their roles and duties overlap? Or were druids and bards essentially the same? No one's sure.

Today, when people hear the word *bard*, they picture

someone like Shakespeare, or perhaps they picture medieval minstrels, strolling through cobblestone streets, strumming their lyres and singing pretty tunes. But these images, which come from comparatively recent times, obscure what the term *bard* meant to earlier centuries, and they dilute the important spiritual roles bards played in ancient Celtic cultures.

Both druids and bards were involved with words—though the words were spoken, not written. But they were far more than primitive poets. They were heralds of kings. They were historians of kingdoms. And beyond these roles, they were believed to have spiritual powers as well. Part prophet, part soothsayer, bards and druids had not only extensive learning but supernatural power. More than mere literary figures, druids and bards were seen as lightning rods for spiritual power, conduits through which flowed a supernatural wisdom.

As we've seen, the Celts saw no firm divisions between the natural and supernatural realms. And the druids and bards straddled these two worlds, using their words to bring harmony out of chaos.

Blessings of eloquence

One of the most frequently visited sites in Ireland is County Cork's famous Blarney Castle. Built in the 1400s and looking somewhat worse for wear, the castle is home to the Stone of Eloquence, better known as the Blarney Stone. Surprising numbers of tourists subject themselves to a rather rigorous and uncomfortable ordeal to kiss the stone. First they must climb stairs to a parapet. Then, they need to get down on the ground, roll over and lay on their backs, and extend their heads to kiss the stone's underside. That's a lot of work, but there's a centuries-old legend promising that anyone who does so will get the gift of gab. As one nineteenth-century clergyman put it: "There is a stone there that whoever kisses/Oh! he never misses to grow eloquent."

Eloquence—that rare ability to marry just the right words to a sentiment and move listeners—appears to have been a gift that some ancient Celts possessed in abundance. And those who didn't have it themselves honored and admired it in those who did. And even though the Celts are remembered as a rough and warring race, they believed that eloquence was more powerful than brute physical strength.

As with other facets of the Celtic world, exceptional expressiveness was seen as a gift of the gods. In particular, verbal ability was respected as a blessing of the deity Ogmios, who was honored as the god of eloquence among the otherworldly divinities. This gift was to be used to serve not only kings and chiefs, but the gods themselves. And legends tell us of the many times the bards rose and spoke divinely sanctioned words to the people.

Unfortunately, we don't have any recordings of their work, let alone any collections of their writings. Instead, druids and bards passed their learning on to the next generations through oral teaching and repetition. It was Romans and Christians who first recorded the amazing tales of these unique literary/spiritual figures, and it was by these records that the valuable and irreplaceable work of this early civilization was kept from vanishing from the earth.

It's a sure thing that reading printed collections of old Irish legends is nothing like what it would have been like to sit in a smoky banqueting hall, gnaw on a pork bone, and listen as the legend-spinners unloaded their highly trained memories. Out came elaborate poetry full of heroic deeds, linked together by acrostics and other devices that help the tale-spinners memorize hundreds of lines of verse.

The really good bards improvised on their huge body of knowledge, filling their language with all sorts of intriguing embellishments, puns, riddles, exaggerations, and hyperbole. This rapid-fire rhetoric was the verbal equivalent of Celtic art's dizzying motifs of interlacing decoration. Or as Anne Ross puts it, the Celts had a deep love of regularity that resulted in "pattern in art, pattern in words, and pattern in song." The result was powerful prose that both entertained and elevated those who heard it, and in the process, the speakers insured that they would have jobs the next day.

🔯 Born to speak

Bards were born to speak, and thankfully, they were born into a culture that valued their contributions and kept them occupied. When they weren't busy singing the praises of the king, there were plenty of other ways they could use their gifts. One of their tasks was to lament the dead, reciting a record of the deceased's deeds and possibly officiating at the funeral. They were also kept busy composing and performing songs for some of the many warriors who defended the tribe. As historian Gerhard Herm writes, "These warriors wanted to be talked about." Once, when a druid prophesied that a warrior would have a long life, the warrior replied: "If it makes me famous, a single day of life would be enough."

The bards were glad to oblige, composing a large body of work that praised the skillful deeds of some of the better-known Celtic warrior heroes. According to Celtic scholar Robert O'Driscoll, "The hero is one who responds to emotion and the impulses of life, to whatever is most immediate and most pressing, and yet he retains control of his destiny in this world." Although strong and valorous, such heroes could be vulnerable, and they were capable of losing a battle or two, but still they rose above the masses through their superior courage and character.

Taking such heroic exploits one step farther, some bards created a literature of larger-than-life superheroes whose legends described them as the children of an otherworldly father and a human mother. Stories about these heroes show them going from victory to victory, invincible in battle. Often these figures were endowed with supernatural powers, and the only way their enemies could bring them down was through chicanery or sorcery.

Many of the Celtic sagas focus on a particular family of divinities. One family that figures prominently in the sagas is that of Lugh, who was acclaimed for his skill as a warrior and a craftsman and the father of Cuchulain, one of the most famous of Celtic heroes. When Cuchulain was born he was named Setanta, but like so many of the legendary heroes, he gained a new name as a result of one of his earliest deeds. He accidentally killed the fierce hound of Culainn, a blacksmith. To repay the smith, Setanta agreed to guard the man's forge until another dog could be found. As a result he was renamed Cuchulain, or "hound of Culainn."

Cuchulain pursued Emer as his wife, and he won her hand from her father after receiving training from a renowned wise man. He fathered one son, but accidentally killed him, showing that heroes could be tragic figures as well as victors. Aside from these setbacks, he was renowned for his exploits on the battlefield. Like his father, Lugh, Cuchulain wielded a powerful spear that could inflict a fatal deathblow on his enemies. But he was even more famous for a maneuver called the salmon-leap, a gravity-defying ability to leap over physical obstacles. Some of the scenes from Cuchulain's battles are replete with Technicolor gore and bosom-heaving romance. Blood spurts from his head, his body contorts in unusual shapes, and he is occasionally surrounded by naked women. In one of his biggest challenges, he battles a club-carrying giant and is proclaimed the supreme champion of Ulster at his victory.

But legendary figures didn't need a battle to inspire them to poetic heights. It was tragedy that moved Amairgin, a member of the Milesians, mythical warriors who came to Ireland from Egypt and Spain. According to the legends, it was one Thursday on May Eve when White-knee and the other Milesians landed on Ireland's soil. But once there, disaster struck. Scene the Shapely, Amairgin's lovely wife, died and was buried near the harbor. Then, Amairgin was overcome with emotion and

eloquence, setting his right foot upon the land and ut-
tering the following song, which is found in Caitlín and
John Matthews' *The Encyclopedia of Celtic Wisdom*:

> I am a wind on the sea,
> I am a wave of the ocean,
> I am the roar of the sea,
> I am an ox of seven exiles,
> I am a hawk on a cliff,
> I am a tear of the sun,
> I am a turning in a maze,
> I am a boar in valor,
> I am a salmon in a pool,
> I am a lake on a plain,
> I am a dispensing power,
> I am a spirit of skillful gift,
> I am a grass-blade giving decay to the earth,
> I am a creative god giving inspiration.

And that was just the first stanza! Following verses included a variety of questions and ruminations on natural
and supernatural phenomena, as well as a spell that was
designed to encourage fish to swim into the harbor "like
a torrent of birds."

Legends like those of Cuchulain and Amairgin were
passed on from bard to bard for centuries, until they
were recorded by Christian monks and scribes. It's impossible for us to know how many of these primitive
tales are based on fact and how many are pure flights of
fancy. But regardless of what inspired them, the bards
helped craft enduring legends that have kept alive the
mythos of the Celtic hero for centuries. And in the

process, they've achieved immortality for themselves, for, as one scholar puts it, they are "the earliest voices from the dawn of Western civilization."

❖ Druidic schools

Before children grow very old, they begin to remember those important dates when presents come, such as birthdays and Christmas. Later, when young people get their first jobs, they will remember a series of numbers that will accompany them all their lives: their nine-digit social security number. Such exercises are only a prelude to adulthood, when one must regularly digest a stream of digits: home and office phone and fax numbers, security codes, checking account numbers, e-mail addresses, and so much more.

Thousands of years ago, it was the druids who demonstrated how amazing the human memory could be. They stored away hundreds, even thousands, of stanzas of versical wisdom, history, and lore in their overstuffed brains. Ironically, their practice of committing everything to memory instead of writing it down led Roman writers to conclude that the druids were illiterate. But according to Ellis, the absence of written works signaled not an ignorance of the art of writing but a religious prohibition against it, "in order that such knowledge should not fall into the wrong hands."

Unlike contemporary theologians, the druids didn't have shelves full of scriptures, commentaries, and manuals. Their wisdom was inscribed in their memory and students wishing to follow their way of life were required to study for twelve to twenty years. Even though that was a demanding curriculum, there were apparently many druidic schools throughout Ireland. One famous community of female druids was allegedly headquartered at Kildare, the site where the Celtic saint Brigid later founded her Christian community.

In their schools, druids-to-be memorized hundreds and hundreds of verses containing the legend and lore of the land. Although this was a massive amount of material to manage, the students were helped by the same kinds of things that help people memorize poetry today: rhythms, rhymes, and the letters that begin each line. It is believed that many of the verses began with letters that spelled out complex acrostics and helped the druids and their students to memorize them more easily. And though we may desperately wish that we knew the content of some of these lessons, they have been lost through time.

❈ Modern revivals

One of the strangest chapters in the long history of druidism happened in 1963 at Carleton College in Northfield, Minnesota, when a group of students tried to find a creative way of getting around the school's regulations requiring attendance at chapel. One of the few loopholes in the chapel regulations was the clause that allowed students to be excused if they attended services of their own religion. The students seized on that clause with glee, and playfully created a new organization that they dubbed the Reformed Druids of North America.

According to Margot Adler, whose book *Drawing*

Down the Moon is a fascinating report on the contemporary Western revival of neo-pagan beliefs and practices, the joke was given an air of authenticity in the group's so-called "Early Chronicles," written in a mock-biblical style. But a funny thing happened to the Reformed Druids of North America: They evolved into a bonafide religious group that actually sponsors ritual celebrations of ancient Celtic holidays. As Adler says, "Once the initial protest was over, the most important aspect of Reformed Druidism had to be that it put people in touch with a storehouse of history, myth, and lore."

▨ Keeping legends alive

If you're looking for a nearby druidic school, you'll search the Yellow Pages in vain. But there are other ways you can keep the spirit of the bards and druids alive today.

- **Tell your own story.** Buy a notebook or a journal and start recording what happens to you during the course of your days. Journaling has become a popular activity, and there are several books that can help you start the practice. For many, this type of inner exploration has become a spiritual exercise. You may not wield big weapons on a mythical battlefield, but you have your share of victories and defeats, and recording them can help you keep track of your own growth and development.
- **Help others tell their stories.** Everybody has a story to tell, but few people actually listen. You can change

that by practicing intentional listening. As you pay attention to what people around you are saying, you'll understand their lives better, and you'll get a front-row seat to the exciting exploits of undiscovered heroes and heroines.

- **Recapture the heroic.** Bards and druids thrived in the Celts' heroic society. People still need heroes to encourage them, inspire them, and show them the way. If you don't have any, perhaps you could spend some time reading biographies of historic figures who, even if flawed and imperfect, may exhibit some of the virtues and characteristics that help them stand out from the crowd.

4

SEEING THE WORLD
AS HOLY

*Behind your image, below your words, above your
thoughts, the silence of another world waits.*

—John O'Donohue, *Anam Cara*

IN AMERICA'S DRY AND rocky southwest, at a place
called Four Corners, you can see four states, and if
you stretch yourself a little, you can put your right hand
on Colorado, your left hand on Utah, your left foot on
Arizona and your right foot on New Mexico. In the
Celtic world, there aren't such nice, neat, geometric-
shaped states. All the dividing lines between ancient
tribal areas or modern-day counties are erratic, following
the contours of the land, the centuries-old divisions between various kingdoms, or even the path of a meandering stream (or a meandering cow). Instead, the Celts
believed that there was another dividing line that all people could straddle, if only they stretched themselves a
bit. And that's the divide between this world and the
"otherworld."

Two basic beliefs were held nearly universally by the Celtic people, no matter where they were during their centuries of migrations throughout Europe. First, they believed that the supernatural pervades all of life. And as a consequence, they believed in a second concept: that the world was full of sacred sites where one could experience, or access, this otherworldly power.

Often, people think of the supernatural as somehow above or beyond the natural world they inhabit, that transcendent means separate. But the Celts believed the spiritual was commingled with the physical, and that their world was simultaneously inhabited by two different kinds of beings: the living and the dead, the visible and the invisible. Instead of seeing the material world and the otherworld as divided by an impenetrable barrier or a great chasm that could only be crossed by the occasional and unusual divine visitation, they believed that the temporal and eternal were as close as the borders of adjoining states, and they were convinced that there was regular traffic between the here and there, the known and the not-so-well-known.

The Celts believed that specific physical sites were particularly convenient portals between the worlds. They referred to these as the "thin places," where the traffic between the worlds was thought to be especially heavy. Some thin places were sacred natural landscapes. Others were holy places of human construction, such as tombs like Newgrange, stone circles like Stonehenge, or hundreds of smaller sacred sites scattered all over Europe. Whether the Celts stood in the middle of a stone circle, or recited incantations in a wild grove, they felt that the gods were close at hand, that they and the divine were one.

🌀 Down with dualism

The Celts' belief that the supernatural pervaded all of life was consistent with their philosophical outlook, which couldn't be more different from the world view that has undergirded Western societies for centuries. Most of us in the West, whether we know it or not, are dualists. Our view of the world has been shaped by the Greek philosopher Plato, a student of Socrates and a teacher of Aristotle. Plato lived about the same time the Celts were beginning to spread out through Ireland, but he and the Celts couldn't have been further apart in the way they understood how the cosmos worked.

Plato viewed the soul and the world of ideas as immortal and eternal. But the human body and the physical world were seen as temporal and fleeting. Centuries later, when the Christian faith began to move beyond its Jewish roots and Middle Eastern origins, it increasingly encountered Platonic philosophy. In time, Christian thinkers declared Christian theism and Platonism compatible, adapting Plato's body-versus-soul dualism to the new faith's teaching about time and eternity, sin and salvation, heaven and hell. In the West, Plato's thought has continued to influence Christian theology to our own day.

The Celts, whose roots were in the East, saw the world in terms of unity not duality, harmonies not discontinuities. For them, the world and everything in it was part of the essential oneness of the gods and nature, the physical and spiritual realms. When they looked at the world, they saw a numinous aura that enlightened and warmed everything before them. Every hill was holy. Every tree and every blade of grass could be the dwelling place of a deity. Each person was good and full of promise.

The Celts didn't hold things that were "religious" or "spiritual" in a separate category from everything else, and in a sense the goal of life wasn't to be more religious, but to be more alive, more awake and sensitive to the divinity believed to be pulsing throughout the universe. Seamus Heaney, the Nobel Prize–winning twentieth-century Irish poet, writes about the "sudden apprehension of the world as light." The Celts knew that light, and it illumined everything they saw.

The Celts' view of the essential unity of all existence helps explain some of their lasting myths and legends. Shape-shifting heroes, traveling between worlds, are able to transform themselves into animals and back again, while the mysterious Selkies swim in the ocean like seals but also have the ability to shed their skins and transform themselves into humans. The skeptic may look at these legends as childish fantasy, but such doubts neglect the deeply held Celtic view that everything is somehow related. For followers of Plato, the physical world is a mere shadow of the ideal realm. For the Celts, the physical world was a place of true vitality, beauty, and spirit.

▦ Wellsprings of the sacred

Water is a sacred symbol in many faiths, from the Hindus' ritual baths in the sacred Ganges River to the Christians' baptismal font, and for the Celts water was an especially potent symbol. The sites where water met land were seen as thin places where humans could connect more directly with invisible spiritual forces. Beaches and shorelines were believed to be sacred sites, and people who sat near a place where water intersected land could receive special wisdom or guidance. In Ireland, subdivided by rivers, dotted by lakes, and surrounded by the sea that washes up against the land in hundreds of bays, such thin places were numerous.

Individuals could also expect to meet the deities near a sacred spring or well. Celtic holy wells weren't the deep, stone-lined circular shafts into which one might drop a bucket. Instead, the Celts venerated natural springs and built shrinelike structures around the places where these springs emerged from the ground. Such practices are not uncommon elsewhere in the world. Wells are venerated in India and Africa, and the Romans built water shrines wherever their empire spread, with one of the more famous examples being Bath in southwestern England. But in some areas of Ireland, the veneration of wells has persisted to the present day, a testimony to how powerful a belief this was for the Celts.

Anyone who's gone for a few hours without a drink knows how beautiful a trickle of water looks, and how good it feels on a parched throat. In addition to these natural benefits, the Celts believed that springs were the sites of unusually heavy activity from otherworldly visitors. They built shrines around them, left offerings in their pools, and bathed both newborn children and dying elders in their cool, clear waters. Some wells were believed to convey healing power, and clay from their banks was used to prevent illnesses. Stone slabs near the wells were used as chairs or couches for people to sit or lie near these healing waters. Some of these stones still show the wear and tear resulting from the trampling of thousands of feet over the course of centuries. For the early Celts, these wells were their family doctors, providing the only "medical" option some poor rural people had.

The importance of these sacred sites didn't wane as Christianity spread. Wells were named after Christian saints, and while nearly all of the hundreds of Celtic saints have at least one well named after them, some have dozens. Holywell, in northern Wales, is dedicated to St. Winefride (or Gwenfrewi in Welsh) and illustrates the continued impact of sacred wells on the Celtic landscape. According to legend, the saint was visited by a man who came to her parents' house for a drink of water, and after quenching his thirst he turned his attentions to Winefride. After she refused his advances, he pursued the young woman to a nearby chapel with his sword drawn. He lunged at her and as her head fell to the ground, a spring of fresh water appeared. Fortunately, the saint's severed head was later reattached to her body, enabling her to found a convent of nuns before her death.

To an outsider, it might be difficult to sort through such legends, or even to tell whether a particular well is

pagan or Christian. Oftentimes, there was little difference between the two in the rituals performed at the
wells or the expectations of the crowd. Under Christian
sponsorship, the wells were visited most frequently on
saints' feast days, during which their water was said to be
unusually powerful.

✾ A year of celebrations

If the Celts believed strongly in sacred places where
humans and deities could meet, they also believed in sacred seasons and organized their lives around four sacred
festivals. Many of these festivals continue to be celebrated throughout the world today, revealing the enduring legacy of these ancient Celtic practices.

Samhain, which is celebrated on November 1, is
the Celtic New Year. One might wonder why a rural,
agricultural-based people like the Celts would celebrate
the New Year at a time when the cool, crisp days of fall
turn into the cold, harsh weather of winter, but Samhain
marks the end of one agricultural year and the beginning
of another. To the urbanite, winter appears to be a time
when nature shuts down, but the Celts, attuned to the
invisible work of nature that continued under the surface
calm, knew the seeds for the next year's crops were busy
germinating. While plants used their dormant period to
grow deep roots, animals hibernated, relying on their
own energy stores until the coming warm weather.

To the Celts, Samhain was more than a celebration of
these invisible activities. Though it was a declaration of
faith that another spring and summer would follow the

harsh winter, the holiday was also believed to be a time when the usually thin barriers between this world and the otherworld all but disappeared. The living mingled freely with the spirits of deceased ancestors, or as Caitlin and John Matthews write, "It is the night on which the faery-hills are opened, when the way between the worlds is very busy with otherworldly traffic, when spirits abound."

Unlike most peoples of the world, who define days as beginning and ending at midnight, the Celts' day began at sundown. So all the Samhain celebrations began on the preceding night, which for us is the last night of October, and the occasion for our celebration of Halloween.

Before Samhain evolved into Halloween, it became the Christian holiday of the All Hallows' Eve, better known as All Saints' Day. This evolution is just one of numerous examples of how Christian traditions embraced and adapted preexisting pagan traditions, in this case substituting deceased saints for deceased ancestors.

Today, remnants of the ancient Celtic holiday of Samhain are still with us. Although they've been homogenized and commercialized, many contemporary pagans still reenact ancient rituals. And in recent years, Halloween has become a more significant celebration on most Americans' calendars. Today, they spend more on Halloween than they do any other holiday, except Christmas. And there are more parties celebrating Halloween than any other event except for New Year's Eve and the Super Bowl.

Imbolc was celebrated February 1, a time when the

snows of winter were tapering off, sunshine was increasing, and some plants and animals were beginning to show signs of renewed life. Because Imbolc was not as important as Samhain, we know less about the meanings and rituals first associated with it. But it is believed it was a time for banishing winter and preparing for the arrival of spring.

As with other pagan holidays, Imbolc was adapted by the Christians, who provide more information about that transition. In the sixth century, the church absorbed Imbolc into the feast of Candlemas, marking the end of Christmas observations (which had started forty days previously) and a celebration of the Virgin Mary. In addition, February 1 became the feast day of St. Brigid, born into a long line of pagan priests and priestesses and later becoming Ireland's most beloved female saint.

In the nineteenth and twentieth centuries, one could still see an intriguing mix of pagan and Christian elements in the Scottish Highlanders' celebrations on February Eve. Many people placed small beds made of cornstalks and grass near the doors to their houses. These beds, sometimes accompanied by burning candles, were symbolic invitations to Brigid to enter their homes and help prepare for the coming spring.

Beltane, celebrated May 1, was second in importance to Samhain in the Celtic calendar, but the celebrations of Beltane were always more joyous, since it marked the beginning of summer. For these ancient agrarian people, the return of warm weather was a cause for gladness. Farmers returned to their fields after a winter of relative inactivity, and animals were put out to pasture after spending months in barns or their caretakers' houses.

As a fertility festival, Beltane was also famous for its effect on human behavior. People had spent months cooped up, too, but now they could spend more time out of doors, renewing acquaintances with distant neighbors, or attending gatherings of their local tribe or kingdom. Couples—both married and not—would pair up and retire to the fields, where their lovemaking was believed to help stimulate the fertility of the natural world. In addition, celebrations would include exuberant (and sometimes erotic) dancing and singing. Perhaps such celebrations help explain why Imbolc, which comes nine months later, is traditionally associated with midwifery.

Perhaps because of its sensual trappings, Beltane wasn't embraced by Christians the same way the other major pagan festivals were. Instead, the holiday was the occasion for St. Patrick to engage Ireland's druids in a kind of spiritual duel. For pagans, one of the traditions of Beltane Eve was the lighting of a ceremonial fire. All the households throughout the land would snuff out their hearth fires and wait in darkness until the Beltane fire was lit on the top of the Hill of Tara. This fire was believed to rid the lands of the ghosts of winter as well as any winter diseases, and from this one fire, the house fires throughout the whole region were to be relit. But one Beltane Eve, Patrick challenged the whole celebration by lighting his own fire on the Hill of Slane, which was clearly visible to the pagans celebrating on the Hill of Tara. Patrick's fire was meant to represent the light of Christ and serves as a symbol of the tensions and confrontations that would long divide the adherents of the old pagan faith from the proponents of the new Christian one.

Throughout Britain, one can still find Beltane celebrations, many of which continue relatively unchanged since ancient days. In some British towns, villagers create an elaborate Jack-in-the-Green costume, which is worn by a local who is often accompanied through the streets by his Green Men. Every year, hundreds of people from around the world travel to Castleton, in northern England, for Garland Day as the villagers help decorate the Garland King, who is covered with flowers and paraded through the town on a horse. Many of us throughout the rest of the world celebrate the remnants of these ancient events in our May Day celebrations. While more traditional rites call for the selection of a May King and May Queen, or gleeful dances around the May Pole, in its more Christian observance the Virgin Mary is the Queen of the May.

Lughnasadh, also known as Lammas, was the fourth of the major Celtic holidays, observed on August 1. As the commemoration of Lugh, the Celtic sun god, Lughnasadh is a joyous summer celebration of the first grain harvest (the gathering of fruits and butchering of meat would come later). Some of the grain was ground into flour and cooked in hearty bread, while the rest was brewed into ale or mead as the people heartily celebrated the bounty of nature. There usually followed a series of banquets in which the villagers ended months of cautious survival on last year's grain and began consuming fresh produce. These gatherings, which signified abundance, frequently included various contests and competitions.

These pagan festivals were important rituals for the ancient Celts, calibrating their lives to the cycles of nature and the workings of the supernatural through the changing of seasons and the tides of want and plenty. They proved remarkably resilient as their forms were adapted to the Christian calendar and were as important in their day as our celebrations of Christmas and Easter.

▨ The nearness of God

Like the pagan belief that the supernatural pervades all of life, the Christian concept of the immanence of God holds that God is both transcendent (above human affairs) and indwelling (involved in human life). The two concepts hang in balance, painting a picture of a deity who is extraordinary, but not so extraordinary as to be unconcerned or uncomprehending of our sorrows and joys. But in part because of its entanglements with Platonic dualism, the theology of the Christian West has typically emphasized God's transcendence, or separation from us. This results in a theology that portrays God as the creator of the universe rather than its sustainer, as a righteous judge of human sins rather than a loving forgiver, more enraged about the state of human affairs than involved in straightening them out.

But when early Christianity came to Celtic lands, it wasn't encumbered by Platonic dualism, and the result was a flowering of Celtic Christianity that is still admired for its spiritual depth, its love for creation, and its near total absence of sanctimony and self-righteousness. Some scholars argue that this emphasis on the immanence of God was unconscious, an artifact of the spiritual and philosophical culture in which the Celtic Christians emerged. Others say it was conscious, the result of an intentional effort to bridge the gaps between pagan and Christian belief systems by emphasizing apparent similarities. In truth, it was probably both. Patrick, who grew up in Roman Britain, may have worked harder than others to meld the two traditions, but the hundreds of Celtic monks and saints who followed him were moved from their own intuitive experience of the closeness of God.

As a result, the writings of the Celtic church are full of references to a personal experience of the divine, whether communing with the saints in prayer, depending on the timely help of angels, or sensing the closeness of God in all of life. John O'Riordain, a contemporary Irish monk, writes that the Celtic Christians lived in a "densely inhabited world of the angels and saints" in which there was "no impassable boundary" between heaven and earth. "The world of angels and saints [was] stronger and even more real than the tangible earthly elements."

Yeats: Friend of Fairies

William Butler Yeats (1865–1939), one of the twentieth century's finest poets, was also an acclaimed playwright and an ardent Irish nationalist who fought not only for Irish independence but for a revival of interest in Gaelic and Celtic arts, literature, legends, and language.

Less well known is his deep interest and involvement in the occult, a facet of this complex man that led writer Stephen Brown to call Yeats "a latter-day pagan." Yeats rejected orthodox religion and instead studied and experimented with a variety of esoteric practices: He married a medium and spiritualist, joining her in trances and automatic writing sessions; he was a disciple of Madame Blavatsky, founder of the Theosophical Society, and also spent time in London with Aleister Crowley, the celebrated Black Magic "priest" and author of books on magic and the occult.

Yeats's eclectic beliefs provided him with a philosophy and a system of symbols that he used in his plays, such as *Purgatory*, and his poems, such as "Byzantium," "Leda and the Swan," and others. But Yeats's beliefs are explained more clearly in such prose works as *The Celtic Twilight*, in which he describes a personal encounter he had with fairies from the otherworld, creatures he once described as "nations of gay creatures, having no souls; nothing in their bright bodies but a mouthful of sweet air."

According to Yeats, during his twenty-seventh year he went to the Rosses, an area renowned for its otherworldly activity. There, as he writes:

> I made a magical circle & invoked the fairies. . . . Once there was a great sound as of little people cheering and stamping with their feet away in the heart of the rock. The queen of the troop came then—I could see her—& held a long conversation with us & finally wrote in the sand "be careful & do not seek to know much about us."

Yeats had a fascination with the otherworld and fairies for the rest of his life. His book *Fairy Tales of Ireland* includes nearly two dozen legends he collected during his travels. In some of the stories, fairies are kindly and gentle. In others, they play despicable tricks on their human victims. In most modern retellings of fairy lore, the positive side of fairies usually predominates over their fearsome side.

In one of his sermons, Columba, the founder of the island monastery of Iona, spoke of the immanence of

God. "Yet of His being who shall be able to speak," he asks. "Of how He is everywhere present and invisible, or of how He fills heaven and earth and every creature, according to that saying, Do I not fill heaven and earth? . . . Heaven is my throne, but earth is my footstool." The same sentiment is expressed in a more homely manner in the traditional Irish blessing, "May God hold you in the palm of his hand, and not squeeze!" or as Andrew Greeley writes, "May you be as close to God as God is to you."

As a result of their emphasis on the immanence of God, the Celtic Christians spent less time arguing about theology than they did seeking direct experience of the Creator, whom they called "the God of life." The communion of saints was a daily reality, not simply a creed. St. Cuthbert, in particular, spent hours in prayer and frequently saw visions of God or spoke with angels. Dead saints were believed to pray for the living, and the dead and the living could communicate, particularly at burial places, which Christians believed were thin places, much as their pagan predecessors had. As one scholar put it, "the saints penetrated every aspect of a person's life."

Today, thousands of people from around the world travel to Ireland every year to experience the presence of the divine firsthand. They're visiting neither the site of an ancient pagan monument nor the grave of a Celtic saint, but Knock, a once-peaceful village in County Mayo's Connemara region, where in 1879, the Virgin Mary allegedly appeared to more than a dozen people. Ever since, Knock has remained one of Europe's most renowned Marian shrines, along with

Lourdes in France and Fatima in Portugal. It only grew in popularity after Pope John Paul II visited and held a Mass for 450,000 people in 1979. Now, with one and a half million visitors every year, Knock is Ireland's busiest tourist destination.

While many pilgrims see Knock as the modern equivalent of an ancient holy shrine, and the crowds that assemble there on important feast days and celebrations as the latest incarnation of the Celtic hunger for the divine, others are more critical. Liam Fay, an Irish journalist, calls Knock "a bizarre and distasteful place" and criticizes the display of "Knock knickknacks," as well as an overall air of commercialization.

While one man's superstition may be another man's sustenance, one thing is clear: The abiding faith in an immanent God survives in the Celtic consciousness. In *Angela's Ashes*, Frank McCourt recounts that as a child, he often talked with an angel who would visit the steps in the family's small flat: "I know he's there because the seventh step feels warmer than the other steps and there's a light in my head. I tell him my troubles and I hear a voice. Fear not, says the voice."

▩ practicing the presence of God

Here are some ideas that might help you practice the presence of God in your daily life.

- **Know what you believe.** In some ways, everyone's a philosopher and a theologian. Are you a Platonic dualist, or are your beliefs closer to those of the Celtic pantheist? Do you believe that our world is routinely invaded by the sacred, or do you think we're hermetically sealed off from the divine? Do you know what you believe and why? Write down your beliefs about humanity, nature, and the cosmos, and examine them critically. Do your beliefs make sense? Continue to examine what you think and believe. Let go of ideas that contradict your experience. Hold fast to what is true.

- **Act out your beliefs.** If you believe in something supernatural, do you live out your faith? Do you consciously invoke God, and actually practice being spiritually sensitive so God can guide and direct you? Such simple but profound practices illustrate the difference between an intellectual religion and a lived faith. Practice practicing what you believe. Open a window in your soul through which God can touch your life.

- **Celebrate the seasons.** Many people's lives revolve around a series of mundane dates and deadlines. For example, millions of Americans dread April 15, while others are bound in perpetual servitude to monthly deadlines for rents or mortgages, utilities, and credit card bills. The Celts had deadlines, too, but they never got so bogged down in such matters that they forgot to joyously celebrate the return of summer with gala feasts and gatherings. Perhaps your world would grow bigger if you kept a closer eye on the cycles of the natural world. Keep track of when the robins return to your garden in the spring. Watch for the budding of the trees, the ripening of their fruit. Allow time every fall to take a stroll through a park

or forest full of fallen leaves. Instead of merely curs-
ing snow, walk through it and listen to it crunch
underneath. Experience nature in all its seasonal
variations.

5

MAKING EVERY DAY SACRED

When God made time, he made plenty of it.

—Celtic maxim

WHETHER IT WAS PAGANS honoring the presence of the divine in nature, or Christians praising the transcendent and immanent God, the Celts believed that every minute of every day was a new opportunity for experiencing the majesty of creation. These "everyday mystics" were deeply aware that the physical world they inhabited and experienced through the five senses was interpenetrated by the supernatural world. And they experienced this reality in a way that was natural without being commonplace.

The difference between the mystical experience of the Celts and the remoteness many moderns feel from God can be seen partly as a result of the world each group inhabits. The Celts lived in small rural villages populated by their kin. They lived closely with their neighbors and the land, and access to the tribal chief or even the local king was easy. Today it is difficult to get another human being to answer the phone, much less to feel that we have a say in our public lives. Our much-hyped communications age has come up with fast and efficient ways to transmit data from one place to another, but in the process has left us feeling alienated from each other and from God. In contrast, our ancient Celtic ancestors felt a closeness to each other as well as an easy intimacy with the spirit world.

This unquestioning acceptance of the presence of the divine in the details of daily life explains why some would gladly walk twenty miles to a church or shrine. The long walk was seen as a time of spiritual preparation, the journey as part of the destination. Spiritual truth and power were in the very air the Celts breathed. This natural mysticism made Celtic spirituality unique, and it's a significant reason why it remains attractive to many today.

▒ "The music of what happens"

According to the logic of Celtic spirituality, if the divine is ever-present, then everything partakes of the divine. Such a view fosters an appreciation and enthusiasm for ordinary life that baffles us today. Monk and author John O'Riordain calls such easy acceptance of life "the music of what happens."

From the world of the fairy tale to the histories of the Celtic saints, there's amazing unanimity about this extraordinary appreciation for the ordinary. The lives of many saints are full of so many miracles and supernatural feats that it seems the saints' feet rarely touch the ground, but a charming episode from the life of an ordinary saint belies this misconception. Lady Gregory relates that, "There was a man going home from Kinvara one night having a bag full of oats on the horse. And it fell and he strove to lift it again but he could not, for it was weighty. Then the saint himself, Saint Colman, came and helped him with it, and put it up again for him on the horse." This simple account is a straightforward depiction of an act of Christian compassion. The fact that the scribe noted it among the stories of Colman's life shows that even a small practical act could reveal a saint's holiness and sanctity.

Twentieth-century Irish poet Euros Bowen captures this feeling today. In his poem "Reredos," a priest celebrating the Eucharist momentarily looks out a church window and catches a glimpse of the radiant beauty of the earth, the joy of birds in flight, and the glorious blaze of the sun. And in a moment, the priest blesses nature as he blesses the bread and wine, consecrating all. While the poem may seem merely symbolic to us today, in fact it may also be referring to an intriguing Celtic sacrament.

According to O'Riordain, both Columba and Mael Ruain, Celtic monks from the sixth and eighth centuries respectively, practiced a unique form of communion. First, worshippers consumed the consecrated bread and wine that constitute the heart and soul of the Mass and are believed to be the transubstantiated Body and Blood of Christ. Then, they consumed unconsecrated bread and wine as well. This "double communion," which is still practiced in some churches today, surprised O'Riordain the first time he experienced it, but he came to realize that it represented a "unifying [of] all of life, bringing sacred and secular into one." Far from making the sacraments mundane, as some traditionalists might fear, such gestures have the opposite effect of bringing much of so-called "natural" life into the realm of the sacred.

▧ The sacramentality of daily life

In Christian teaching, a sacrament is a physical act that mirrors a deeper spiritual reality and serves as a vehicle of God's presence and grace. The Celtic Christians' sense of the immanence of God in all areas of their lives led them to sacramentalize nearly every movement of every day. In the process, they created hundreds of prayers and blessings designed to invite divine help and protection into every area of life. Many of these prayers have been gathered for today's readers in the *Carmina Gadelica*.

One might begin the day with the simple prayer— "Thanks to Thee, O God, that I have risen today/To the rising of this life itself"—and end it with a hopeful "I lie down with God,/And God will lie down with me." In between, there are prayers and blessings for almost every imaginable act, such as the "Blessing of the Kindling," which was typically whispered by the wife as she started the fire at the break of day:

> I will kindle my fire this morning
> In the presence of the holy angels of heaven . . .
> God kindle Thou in my heart within
> A flame of love to my neighbor,
> To my foe, to my friend, to my kindred all.

These prayers weren't simple static traditions, but were clearly transformative. In them we see that the

Celts were concerned with the viewing of every single act—no matter how minute or seemingly mundane—as a sacred opportunity to experience God's radiant grace. Through the simple act of lighting a fire, God was acknowledged and invoked, and a request was made: that God would kindle a fire in a human soul, empowering feeble humanity to live a spirit-directed life until the sun set again. The priest Michael Mitton notes, "Celtic Christians found it as natural to pray during the milking of a cow, as they did in church. . . . Thus there were prayers for getting up in the morning, for washing and dressing, for working, for resting, for meeting friends, for eating, for tidying the house, for undressing, for going to bed." O'Riordain recalls learning a common ritual when he milked his family's cows. Before pointing a cow's udders at the bucket, he would always milk the first couple of strokes onto the ground. While this might be considered a waste, to people raised to believe in the importance of mystery and ritual, it's a powerful symbol of how the notions of sacrifice and thanksgiving pervade nearly all aspects of life.

Mealtime allowed another such opportunity, giving the Celts a chance to thank God for the abundance of the earth while requesting that life be spent pursuing good ends. This "Mode of Taking Food and Drink" comes from an ancient Welsh text, *The Rudiments of Divinity*:

When thy takest thy food, think of Him who gives it, namely, God, and whilst thinking of His Name, with the word put the first morsel in thy mouth, thank God for it, and entreat his grace and blessing upon it, that it may be for the health of thy body and mind; then thy drink in the same manner. And upon any other thing or quantity, which thy canst not take with the Name of God in thy mind, entreat his grace and blessing, lest it should prove an injury and a curse to thee.

There were also prayers and blessings thanking God for the rising of the sun or the shining of the moon, asking relief from headaches or protection from the deadly effects of plague, and much, much more. Today, we too can be more mindful of our everyday acts, drawing on the words of the ancient Celts, or composing our own prayers, to sacramentalize our lives.

🔲 The nectar of life

The lives of Celtic saints are full of simple, life-affirming stories, such as the one about St. Colman helping the man place his sack of oats back on his horse. But in addition to the milk of human kindness, some of the saints' stories run with rivers of beer. The enjoyment of food and drink became another opportunity to demonstrate God's celebration of life.

Many of us are familiar with the first miracle of Jesus, turning water into wine at the wedding feast of Cana. Some fundamentalists and teetotalers insist it was grape juice. But not St. Darerca, also known as Moninna the Abbess. This Celtic saint, who was baptized by St. Patrick, allegedly turned water into wine too.

The miracle took place during her visit to County Louth, "where the dwelling place of her people formerly was." Perhaps Darerca thought these people, who had recently converted to Christianity from paganism, had special need of a miracle to strengthen their new Christian faith since they had been "endowed in ancient times more than the neighboring tribes with skill in the magical arts." But Darerca's main concern was the happiness of the sisters traveling with her, as well as that of another group of Christian women with whom they were lodging. "She, by her own hand," according to legend, "through God's grace, supplied what was deficient in their supplies—that is, drink, fitting for the entertainment of such a company. For she blessed a vessel full of water and God so worked through her that the water was turned into the best of wine."

Not content with this success, the next episode recorded in the saint's life tells how she repaid a neighbor's hospitality by blessing him with beer. One night, as a peasant named Denech was patrolling his fields, he came across Darerca and her sisters, who were traveling at night, for "it was the custom of the spouse of Christ to travel by night rather than by day, so that the sight of the everyday affairs of humanity would not distract her little doves." Denech, a faithful and humble man, invited the weary sisters to his house for food and drink. After eating and drinking, Darerca blessed the house. Then, her eye landed on the pitcher that had been used to serve the sisters beer. It was almost empty, and as the saint blessed the pitcher it was filled to overflowing with enough rich brew to serve all the man's guests. Darerca also blessed the man's property, which greatly increased its bounty.

Even after she had died and "migrated to Christ," a holy well dedicated to St. Darerca continued to produce brew. In the final episode of her legend, St. Finbarr was a guest at the monastery Darerca had founded. While a sister at the monastery was praying to the deceased saint, as he records, containers filled with water "turned into the best beer . . . and there was adequate refreshment for those who drank."

But perhaps no one celebrated life, and thereby honored Christ, more effusively than the beloved St. Brigid. In one of the best-known poems in the Celtic religious tradition, Brigid expresses her intriguing combination of devotion to God and zest for life:

> I should like to have a great pool of ale for the King
> of Kings;
> I should like the heavenly host to be drinking it for
> all eternity.
>
> I should like to have the fruit of Faith, of pure
> devotion;
> I should like to have the couches of Holiness in my
> house.
>
> I should like to have the men of Heaven in my own
> dwelling;
> I should like the vats of Long-Suffering to be at their
> disposal.
>
> I should like to have the vessels of Charity to
> dispense;
> I should like to have the pitchers of Mercy for their
> company.
>
> I should like there to be cheerfulness for their sake;
> I should like Jesus to be there too.

I should like to have the Three Marys of glorious
    renown;
I should like to have the people of Heaven from
    every side.

I should like to be vassal to the Lord;
if I should suffer distress He would grant me a good
    blessing.

For Brigid, as well as the other Celtic saints, life was a
joyful celebration and God's blessings could be made
manifest in something as simple as a mug of beer.

▨ Offerings and exercises

Both pagan Celts and Celtic Christians devised elaborate systems of ritual to access the divine. Though many
of the details of pagan practice are lost to us, archaeologists have helped to unlock some of the mysteries of
their practice.

At numerous pagan sites throughout the Celtic
world, researchers have found the remains of bread cakes,
left at the sacred sites as sacrificial offerings. Such grain
offerings may have been made throughout the year, but
it's clear that they were especially popular during the
four great feasts of Samhain, Imbolc, Beltane, and Lughnasadh and were designed as expressions of thanks to the
gods and goddesses controlling nature and fertility.

Pagan people also made various offerings to the
fairies, or woodland spirits, but it seems that these liba-
tions were less an expression of thanks than they were a

form of insurance. With small food and grain offerings, it was hoped that the mercurial and mischievous sprites might spare humans harm or mischief. Such offerings are probably the origin of the popular Halloween custom of "Trick or Treat."

As Celtic lands became Christian, many of these ancient rituals remained, but their significance changed. The circle was a powerful ritual symbol for pagan people, who covered the Celtic lands with thousands of stone circles and other round monuments, and who worshipped the sun as a most powerful and circular god. Christians also embraced the circle, best seen in the unique Celtic cross. No one is entirely sure why Celts added the circle design to the cross's traditional horizontal and vertical beams. Many see the Celtic cross as ripe with spiritual symbolism, a depiction of Christ's connection to the natural world, through the image of the sun, while at the same time demonstrating his supremacy over the pagan sun god. Others see the circle as a more general symbol of holism and God's all-embracing love for the world. Whatever its original meaning, the Celtic cross remains one of the Celts' most lasting legacies.

Another way Christians incorporated the circle into some of their rituals was through the use of various "encompassing" or "encircling prayers." In some cases, worshippers would begin by standing in place with arms extended. Then, they would turn clockwise ninety degrees, say a prayer invoking divine protection—"My Christ! my Christ! my shield, my encircler/Each day, each night, each light each dark"—and continue turning and rotating as they completed the entire circle. In other cases, believers would pray as they walked in a circuit around their home, a shrine, or some other sacred site.

CELTIC HIGH CROSSES

No symbol says "Celtic Christianity" as clearly as the beautiful Celtic crosses, which one writer described as "prayers in stone."

Pre-Christian Celts had long marked off sacred territory with various sacred stones, columns, and monuments. The Christian Celts were no different. At first, Christians in Celtic lands merely carved cross symbols on existing pagan stones. By the eighth century, monastic artists were busy carving distinctive Celtic crosses. Today, more than a hundred of these crosses survive in Ireland, with hundreds more in Cornwall in England. Many others were destroyed by Protestants who believed the crosses represented Catholic idolatry.

The most distinctive element of the cross is the ring that surrounds the crossbeams. Although some researchers argue that the circle was merely an engineering device designed to hold the weight of the heavy horizontal beams, most people now agree the ring was a symbolic design element. Circles were important spiritual symbols to pagan Celts. Perhaps by combining a cross and a circle the Christians were trying to show the world that they believed Christ to be the center and culmination of all things. The cross also symbolized Christ's lordship over all of creation.

Artists also covered the crosses with extensive, extravagant designs. Some of this design work was abstract and geometrical in style, featuring the same kind of intricate interlacing that decorated Celtic metalwork as well as the artwork on the pages of the Book of Kells.

In addition to this abstract art, many crosses featured numerous panels that were used to display various biblical characters and scenes. The West Cross at Monasterboice in County Louth is Ireland's tallest, which means it has more room for biblical panels. The front side alone has twelve panels, each crammed full of biblical characters and motifs.

Clonmacnoise has many crosses and partial crosses, and it was believed that this monastic center was the home of a major workshop where sculptors turned out crosses for other monasteries throughout Ireland. The Clonmacnoise crosses are famous for their fine, precise design work.

The Cross of the Scriptures is probably the best-known cross at Clonmacnoise. Its weather-worn panels tell the story of Christ's Passion, beginning with the events of Palm Sunday and concluding with the Resurrection on Easter, which takes center stage at the hub of the cross's beams. For many preliterate Celtic believers, these panels were an easy way to grasp important Christian concepts. Also, it appears that many people would circle the crosses on their knees, praying as they kneeled before each panel.

In other parts of the world, Christianity has left a legacy of huge cathedrals and other architectural wonders. The Celtic Christians left behind their crosses, which speak volumes about the beautiful spiritual revolution they wrought.

The use of the circle was also a uniquely Celtic way of expressing a foundational Christian confession: that God is God of all the earth and all of life. Or as scholars Oliver Davies and Fiona Bowie write in *Celtic Christian Spirituality*: "There was no aspect of life which was not in some way touched by the intricate webs of ritual and belief that have life and meaning to the Celtic world."

✠ Trapped in time

Some of the things people find most attractive about Celtic spirituality are its emphasis on everyday sacraments, its extraordinary reverence for the signposts and symbols of the sacred in ordinary life, and its relaxed and easygoing approach to reverence. "I would like to live like that," some might say, "but I just don't have the time." To such quibbling, the Celts might respond with one of their classic maxims: "When God made time, he made plenty of it!"

The Celts viewed time as a plentiful gift of God. They didn't run around in frantic effort to squeeze every ounce of productivity out of each sixty-second interval. And they would be shocked at the capitalist maxim that time is money. As they saw, time was way too valuable to be cheapened by commerce. Instead, the Celtic people viewed time as a finite but abundant resource that was provided for our blessing and enjoyment by the same forces that created the sun, the moon, and the stars.

Cormac Mac Ciolionain, a Celtic king, bishop, and intellectual, wrote poetry and treatises on a variety of subjects, as well as a rule for the monastic community located near his seat of power in Cashel. In his rule, he wrote, "Decorous and unhurried celebration is the crown of every good work, and we have nothing but praise for it," revealing a deep respect for time without bowing to it. It's not that time didn't matter to these people, but somehow they were able to live lives that weren't ruled by the clock. How did they develop an approach to time that's so different from ours?

For the earliest Celts, the only time that mattered was seasonal time. Farmers needed to know when to plant and when to harvest. Wise men told them how to read the signs, and some even officiated at seasonal holidays designed to demarcate these important periods in life. Both Newgrange and Stonehenge, the two most impressive pre-Celtic monuments, were attuned to seasonal cycles.

Every technology carries with it unintended consequences, and the advent of more precisely measured time seems to have brought more than its share. Something that began as a convenience has become a tyrant. Many of us feel that our lives are dictated by the clock and we don't have enough time to do what really matters. And many have taken the "time is money" dictum to an unhappy extreme, working longer hours to get more goodies while skimping on less "valuable" things, such as time talking to spouses, neighbors, and family members.

A saintly Celtic legend may help restore our understanding of time as a plentiful gift of God. According to this tale, Mochaoi of Ulster was out one day with his brothers cutting down timber to build a church. As he was assembling a load of wattles, he heard a beautiful song in the bush nearby. Entranced by the bird's song, he moved closer, and the bird spoke to him, telling Mochaoi he had been sent from God to entertain him. It seemed like a good idea to the saint, who stood listening to the bird for the next three hundred years. When the bird finally bid farewell, it seemed to the saint that less than an hour had passed.

God wants to entertain us all. If only we had the time.

▩ Giving thanks

There's a final and important thing to be said about the Celts and their practice of seeing the sacred in the everyday: They possessed something best described as an attitude of gratitude.

The Celts saw everything in nature around them as wrapped up in the supernatural. Each tree was a colorful reminder of divinity. Each hill a new revelation of the creator's majesty. Each fresh, new morning a promise of God's steadfast love. The Celts didn't question, evaluate, judge, or reject. They accepted what they were given and gave thanks.

O'Riordain recalls Mrs. Neylon, a schoolteacher from his childhood who embodied this. Every morning she would begin the day by saying, "A grand fine morning, thanks be to God." O'Riordain recalls that such sentiments made perfect sense during one of Ireland's many grand and glorious days of sunshine and beauty. But for Mrs. Neylon, giving thanks to God wasn't a sunny-day-only thing. One day, she entered the classroom, her coat and shoes soaked from a lashing rainstorm. As she took her cap off her head and shook it, she proclaimed, "A grand wet morning, thanks be to God."

For the Celts, giving thanks wasn't conditional. It wasn't dependent on sunny skies, a good boss, or a booming stock market. Thankfulness was a way of life. And in the process of giving thanks, the Celts found they had very much to be thankful for.

▦ Seizing the moment

Because they saw sacredness in every moment, the Celts saw opportunities for spiritual growth in each second of every day. Perhaps we can learn something about the true value of time from this ancient wisdom. Here are some ideas to get you started.

• **Sacramentalize your life.** The Celts prayed when they rose in the morning and when they went to bed at night. Perhaps your waking life would be different if you framed it with such prayers. Prayer is extremely portable; you can take it with you anywhere. Prayer is also sublimely simple; you can express yourself to God in a second if that's all the time you have. Why not begin praying when you're stuck in traffic, while you're standing in the grocery store checkout line, or when you're waiting for a meeting to begin? Turn these high-pressure periods into times for tapping into the presence of God in the present moment.

- **Stop and listen to "the music of what happens."** You'll never see the beauty of the world if you're not looking and listening. This isn't an assignment to wear rose-colored glasses. Instead, it's merely a reminder that you may be missing some pretty neat stuff.

- **Be thankful for what you have got.** You may not be the prettiest, tallest, smartest, richest, quickest, or happiest person in the world. But do you have anything going your way? Is there any possession, ability, or relationship that makes you feel the least bit grateful? If so, why not develop an attitude of gratitude. Thankfulness won't turn curmudgeons into saints, but it will help break you out of cycles of cynicism, self-pity, and regret.

- **Take a time out from time.** The Celts felt they had plenty of time. We feel we'll never have enough. Something's changed over the past fifty centuries, but it's not the number of hours or minutes in a day. Why not consider taking some time away from time? Go somewhere—a park, a chapel, or your back porch— and leave your wristwatch behind. Step out of the constraints and pressures of time. If you can, watch the sun or the moon moving across the sky. Focus on the things that are more meaningful than the next pressing deadline. In *Putting First Things First*, Stephen Covey talks about the difference between truly important things and merely urgent things. Begin to make time-away-from-time a regular part of your life.

6

CHRISTIANIZING THE CELTS

Should I be worthy, I am prepared to give even my life
without hesitation and most gladly for His name, and
it is in Ireland that I wish to spend it until I die, if the
Lord would grant it to me.

—St. Patrick

BY THE END OF the fourth century, the Celtic fringes of Ireland, Wales, and Scotland remained virtually untouched by what was then known elsewhere as "civilization." Pagan practices, which had ceased or been supplanted in mainland Europe, were still flourishing in remote, rural Ireland. Into this ragged and rugged world stepped Patrick, who had a profound effect on the conversion of Ireland.

Patrick, who stands at the boundary separating the prehistoric Celts from their historical descendants, is one of the more intriguing people human history has produced. Yet there is rancorous debate about where he traveled, what he did there, whom he converted, and even the dates of his birth and death. And there is well-deserved skepticism about some of the most mythical parts of his legend, such as his banishing snakes from Ireland, or his use of the three leaves of the shamrock to illustrate the theological concept of the Trinity.

But there's one big difference between Patrick and all those who preceded him. Unlike the druids, who believed that writing things down was a cardinal sin, Patrick wrote with a passion. There are two documents we can trace with certainty to Patrick, and as a result, he is really the first Celtic person we can truly approach on his own terms. We will never be sure what prehistoric pagans practiced, or what the druids did, and we'll never be able to separate fact from fantasy in the myths and legends about the Celts' heroes. But with the arrival of Patrick on the scene, we at last have a person whose passions we can feel, whose anxieties we can understand, and whose beliefs we can grab onto.

There can be no doubt that Patrick's preaching and tireless traveling did convert a good portion of Ireland to Christianity. "I am a servant in Christ to a foreign nation for the unspeakable glory of life everlasting which is in Jesus Christ our Lord," wrote Patrick in his "Letter to Coroticus." In the first few centuries after Patrick's death, the island was substantially Christianized, and in time, Ireland sent missionaries throughout the world. But that's getting ahead of ourselves.

▥ Setting the stage

What was it that led so many Celts to embrace Christianity? Was there a breakdown in the culture, or in its pagan belief system? Or was Patrick simply an extraordinary evangelist?

In the parable of the sower, Jesus explained the theology of evangelism in a simple story about a farmer who went out to sow his seed. Some fell along the path, where the birds ate it up. Some fell on rocky ground where it withered away. But some fell on fertile soil, where it took root, blossomed, and produced a bounty. In Ireland, the Christian message fell on some of the most fertile soil it has ever encountered. The Celtic church that blossomed there yielded a bountiful crop that one writer described as "a Christianity so pure and serene as . . . could hardly be equaled and never repeated." What was it about Ireland that made it so receptive to the Christian message?

One answer can be found in the Celts' frustration with the utter unpredictability of their pagan deities, who could shower them with blessings one minute and then curse them with famine the next. Like the Hindu goddess Kali, who was both a beneficent mother figure and a fierce and bloodthirsty goddess of war, Celtic deities could be both heavenly and horrific. "It would be an understatement to assert that the Irish gods were not the friendliest of figures," writes Thomas Cahill, author of *How the Irish Saved Civilization*. Underneath the pleasing face of pagan pantheism were gods and goddesses who presided over a world that was "full of hidden traps," leaving the Celts with an impression that "suggested subconsciously that reality had no predictable pattern, but was arbitrary and insubstantial." Add to this the inherent social instability of a heroic age, with its chieftains and warriors, its intertribal conflicts and rowdy raiding parties, and it's clear that large numbers of Celts were ready for a religious conversion. Many were willing to trade in their unpredictable, impersonal divine forces for the God Patrick proclaimed, a God who was personal, compassionate, and principled.

Andrew Greeley describes the Celts as a "proto-sacramental" people who were "predisposed to Catholic thinking." They had a belief in the immortality of the soul but lacked a clear vision of what the afterlife held. Their pre-Celtic ancestors had erected massive burial monuments like Newgrange, which had a cross-shaped inner chamber, but they never developed a clear-cut theology to match the Christian doctrine of the resurrection. And while Newgrange and Stonehenge were aligned to the sun and the movements of the heavens, Patrick preached a message that linked the mysteries of creation to a majestic Creator. The Celts' natural mysticism and nondoctrinal spirituality made them receptive to Patrick's amazing teachings.

▩ The life of Patrick

The bare facts about the life and ministry of Patrick have been inflated, distorted, and spiritualized until they resemble little more than what one writer called "pious fiction." But behind all the hoopla is a very real human being who, thanks to his own writings, is surprisingly easy for us to understand. While there may be some quibbling over dates and other specifics, there's general agreement about the important details of the life of the patron saint of Ireland.

Patrick, who was called by the Latinized name Patricius in his homeland of Roman-occupied England, was born around 390 to a man named Calpurnius, a Roman tax official and relatively well-to-do landowner. It was a Christian family: Patrick's father was a deacon in a local congregation, and his father's father had been a presbyter, or priest. Patrick probably met the religious requirements laid down by his parents, but there's no indication he was particularly devout. "I did not know the true God," he writes in his *Confession*, which is our most reliable source for most of the details of his life.

Things changed drastically when Patrick was around sixteen. For a century or more, Irish tribes had raided nearby isles in their search for slaves and booty. Now that the Roman Empire was showing signs of decline, and its ability to defend far-flung areas like Britain decreased, the raids there became more frequent. When a group of raiders attacked Patrick's father's small estate, they grabbed the boy, threw him in a ship with hundreds of other Britons, and took him across the water to a mountainous area in the northern half of Ireland, where he worked as a herdsman for a pagan farmer. Separated from his homeland and his loved ones, Patrick found himself among a race of people whose lifestyle and language he couldn't understand. Some would have responded to such circumstances with anger and rebellion. Others would have become frustrated and withdrawn. Patrick prayed. "In a single day I would say as many as a hundred prayers, and almost as many at night," he writes.

Patrick was around twenty-two when he says he received a supernatural vision in which he was told to flee his flocks and get on a boat. "See, your ship is ready," said the voice. After a harrowing two-hundred-mile overland journey and a horrifying series of close calls and delicate negotiations, Patrick was sailing homeward.

Many believe he spent some time in study, either in England or on the continent. At any rate, he returned to his homeland, possibly expecting to settle down: "Again after a few years I was in Britain with my people, who received me as their son, and sincerely besought me that now at last, having suffered so many hardships, I should not leave them and go elsewhere."

But there would be no settled life for Patrick. Instead, he experienced a life-changing vision:

> I saw in the night the vision of a man whose name was Victoricus, coming as if it were from Ireland, with countless letters. And he gave me one of them, and I read the opening words of the letter, which were The voice of the Irish, and as I read the beginning of the letter I thought that at the same moment I heard their voice . . . and thus did they cry out as with one mouth: We ask thee, boy, come and walk among us once more.

Off went Patrick to Ireland again, not in chains in the belly of a slave ship, but captive to nothing except his own passion to follow what he believed to be the unmistakable calling of God.

His official assignment from those who ordained him was to serve as bishop to the small and inconsequential Christian community in Ireland. But before long Patrick was reaching beyond the faithful flock, traveling far and wide to meet, greet, and recruit pagans to his one-man Celtic crusade. In his mission, he could be winsome and downright compelling. His conversation with Ethne and Fedelm, the daughters of the pagan King Loiguire, is a textbook study in evangelistic dialogue, turning the women's questions into an opportunity to deliver a soliloquy on the nature of God: "Who is God, and where is God, and whose God is he, and where is his house?" asked the women. "Give us some idea of him: how he may be seen, how loved; how he may be found."

Patrick replied; Our God is the God of all people, the God of heaven and earth, of the sea and of the rivers, the God of the sun and the moon and of all the stars, the God of the high mountains and of the deep valleys. He is God above heaven and in heaven and under heaven, and has as his dwelling place heaven and earth and the sea and all that are in them. His life is in all things. . . . Truly, now, since you are daughters of an earthly king, I wish that you will believe and I wish to wed you to the king of heaven.

The two daughters believed, were baptized, and began wearing white veils on their heads as a symbol of their dedication to God.

Patrick could also be confrontational, as he was on the Hill of Slane. If you visit the hill, which is an hour north of Dublin, you can see an old graveyard, the remains of a church, and a statue of Patrick, with his hand extended in a peaceful gesture of blessing over the nearby hills and valleys. But things weren't peaceful that Beltane night when Patrick defied pagan practice and lit his own bonfire, which was clearly visible to the druids on the nearby Hill of Tara. "What is this?" asked King Loiguire, the same King Loiguire whose daughters joined with Patrick. "Who is it who has dared to commit this sacrilege in my kingdom? Let him be put to death."

This wouldn't be the last time Patrick would receive death threats from the pagan church-state establishment of his day. But such threats didn't deter this messenger to Ireland:

> . . . should I be worthy, I am prepared to give even my life without hesitation and most gladly for His name, and it is there that I wish to spend it until I die, if the Lord would grant it to me.

🔲 Man with a message

Patrick wasn't the first Christian bishop sent to Ireland. A little-understood man named Palladius had been commissioned earlier, but he apparently lacked Patrick's way with the Irish and had little to show for his efforts. Patrick, who was zealous without being repellent, was the right man for the job. (And this wouldn't be the last time that converting the Celts required just the right man for the job. More than a century later, the monks of Lindisfarne would send Corman to evangelize Scotland. And when the Scots had rejected Corman as too severe, the monks sent the gentle Aidan, who was welcomed with open arms.) Patrick had a warm and gracious manner that made the Irish want to know more about his strange but intriguing ideas about God. Having lived among the Irish for six years, Patrick understood their culture, their mindset, and their hunger for God.

His knowledge of the Celts wasn't something he picked up in a crash course on cross-cultural evangelism.

Patrick knew the hearts of the Irish people. And unlike those Christians who had accompanied the Romans as they spread out and colonized the known world, Patrick didn't come holding a Bible in one hand and a government-issued sword in the other. Patrick's gift to the Irish was "the first de-Romanized Christianity in human history," writes Thomas Cahill. This peaceful, personal approach—we can call it Patrick's gracious evangelism—remains an exemplary model for those who wish to change hearts without exchanging gunfire. Using persuasion instead of coercion, Patrick won a nation to God. "Ireland is unique in religious history for being the only land into which Christianity was introduced without bloodshed," says Cahill. Or as Andrew Greeley writes, "Catholic Christianity slipped into Ireland gently, there were no mass or forced conversions, no bloody battles, no martyrs." Citing two main reasons for Ireland's gentle conversion, Greeley argues, "First, nowhere else in the world did Christianity have enough confidence in itself to take over so completely the symbols of the pagan religion that it encountered than in Ireland. Second, perhaps nowhere else was the pagan religion so easy to assimilate and reinterpret."

As tenth-century Celtic writer Abbot Adso put it, "Hibernia's soil was rich in Christian grace." Or to state it in the language of Jesus' parable of the sower: The seed Patrick had sown grew into a bounteous crop.

🔳 The spread of Celtic Christianity

Some will undoubtedly feel that the phrase "gentle evangelism" is oxymoronic. But Patrick and those who soon followed in his footsteps didn't preach a culturally specific Christianity. They didn't come bringing the gift of the Gospel in one hand and the rule of Roman law in the other. In many ways, theirs wasn't even a Roman Catholic Christianity, as later squabbles with the Roman hierarchy would reveal.

What Patrick gave the Irish was a faith that took the best of traditional pagan beliefs and redefined these in Christian terms. The Celtic Christians didn't tear down and destroy the stone circles and monuments that had been around for ages, as some zealous preachers would do centuries later. Instead they merely inscribed crosses on them alongside the pagan symbols.

The arrival of Christianity wasn't like the inauguration of a new administration, which upon assuming power gets rid of the old cronies and brings in its own set of new cronies. It was more a process of give-and-take. Druids converted and became priests, but they didn't do away with all their former pagan practices overnight. Rather, they augmented their current repertoire of rituals with Christian ones. Sacred wells and shrines to gods and goddesses were rededicated to local holy men and women. Small Christian churches began popping up on traditional pagan sites. And these churches incorporated many Celtic elements, such as decorative touches like sculptures of severed heads, long a sacred image to the Celts, or even the sexually explicit Sheela-na-gig, an ancient fertility goddess. As O'Riordain put it: Over a period of decades, Christians first endorsed, then refined, and finally transcended paganism.

While some may think they made far too many accommodations to paganism, the Christians' strategy turned out to be a stunning success. David Clarke, author of *A Guide to Britain's Pagan Heritage*, writes: "Today it is difficult to locate any purely pagan cult sites in Ireland, for they were all transformed into churches, monasteries, or the burial places of their particular new saint or guardian." As a result of the contextualized manner in which the faith was first proclaimed, the Christianity that flourished in Ireland during the fifth, sixth, and seventh centuries was indigenous, spontaneous, sincere, serious, attractive, hospitable, earth-friendly, and incredibly contagious.

In a little over a century, Ireland was largely transformed from a remote pagan outpost to the "isle of the saints." Not long after the church sent Patrick as a missionary to Ireland, Ireland was sending hundreds of monks and missionaries around the known world. Once Christianized, Ireland re-Christianized the world. This so-called Irish Miracle was a natural consequence of the buoyant beauty of the Celtic Christian experiment. Their cups were filled to overflowing, and the overflow covered much of the world.

Whaҭ Makes a Sainҭ?

When Mother Ҭeresa, a woman many considered a living saint, died in September, 1997, there was an immediate call to have her formally recognized as a saint by the Catholic church.

Church officials, however, responded by

explaining that such things take time.
Declaring someone a saint is a process that
has evolved over centuries. If a person is
martyred serving God, sainthood can come
quickly. If not, the process can't even begin
until five years after the candidate has died,
and there must be sufficient proof of
supernatural miracles and virtuous living.

Celtic Christians didn't bother with such
formalities. They loved and honored thousands
of their holy men and women with the title
"saint," although few of the Celtic saints are
officially recognized as such by the Catholic
church. In *Wisdom of the Celtic Saints*, Edward
Sellner describes the several major stages of
life that are common to many Celtic holy
people.

Even before birth, the saint's distinguished
ancestry is established. Sometimes that required
some creative genealogical research. Then
immediately prior to birth, angels or other
divine agents *foretell* the arrival of the saint on
earth. Often, the birth itself is accompanied by
supernatural miracles.

In order to attain spiritual maturity, the
saint-in-progress finds a *spiritual mentor* for
guidance and counsel. After a time, the saint
"graduates" and becomes a spiritual *mentor to
others*.

The Christian Celts were a *wandering* people,
and saints usually took to the highways or the
high seas to follow God's will and proclaim

God's message. Often, these travels were the occasion for numerous *miracles* that enabled the saints to overcome impossible odds.

Finally came *death*, and often this was foretold by another or intuited directly by the saint. But that wasn't the end of a saint's impact, for even after death, *more miracles* often followed the saint's bones, saintly relics, or prayers to the saint.

Some Celtic saints were honored for their holy lives and charitable deeds. Others were revered for the miracles that accompanied their every step. Still others were renowned for founding some of the many Celtic monasteries that sprang up in Ireland and throughout Europe.

Another group of Celtic saints didn't achieve holiness through any of these routes. These "royal" or "kingly" saints achieved godliness in the crucible of worldly power. According to Nigel Pennick's *The Celtic Saints*, royal saints could achieve sanctity through four basic ways. One, they founded important royal families. Two, they abdicated their earthly thrones for the devout life. Three, they gave land or property to the church. And four, they died in battle against pagan enemies.

Like Patrick, the monks and mystics who propelled the spread of the faith were inspired by a deep desire to see their neighbors know God, and they were often guided by voices and visions. One heavenly vision came to two men simultaneously; Enda of the western Aran Islands and Ciaran, who was visiting him. In the vision, both saw a great tree growing in the middle of Ireland. Its branches protected and shaded the island and provided shelter for a great flock of birds, which carried the tree's fruit across the seas and far beyond the island. The two men interpreted the vision as God's way of telling Ciaran to found his monastery at Clonmacnoise, which was in the center of Ireland. But seen in retrospect, it may have also been a preview of the way in which Celtic Christianity would grow and spread.

🔲 Conflicting cultures

While the Celts warmly embraced the gospel according to Patrick, church leaders in Rome didn't know what to think. Some were curious, some were concerned, and some were convinced that this so-called Celtic spirituality was little more than warmed-over paganism. "The life and practice of the [Celtic Christians] were in many respects unorthodox," wrote the English historian Bede, in a startling example of his knack for understatement. The Celtic Christians weren't anti-Roman. It's simply that they were so unique and original that those used to business-as-usual in the church hierarchy weren't sure what to make of them. There were many obvious cultural contrasts between these two versions of Christianity.

Celtic churches were small, simple structures made of wood and wattle. That was a contrast to the massive and ornate cathedrals of stone built by the Roman church. And these were more than differences in architectural style. Roman buildings symbolized a church that was wealthy and worldly-wise. Irish believers, who were humble and lowly, were much more likely to befriend the impoverished and the destitute than the rich and famous.

The Roman church was bureaucratic and global, while the Celtic church was tribal and local. Like the once highly efficient Roman government, the Roman church kept control of its vast empire through hierarchy and the chain of command. Irish Christianity was more local and monastic in character. Monks often had more credibility and authority than the bishops to whom they officially reported.

Although the two churches affirmed the same creeds, the way they practiced spirituality was radically different. Celtic Christianity was mystical, intuitive, and personal. Celtic monks would spend hours in prayer or a variety of harsh ascetic practices. Meanwhile, Roman Christianity was bureaucratic, law-driven, and efficient, and its officials seemed to spend more hours in high-powered meetings than they did in silence or solitude.

Wild, rustic, and charismatic, the Celtic church was the perfect vehicle to promote Christianity to the Irish. And with their homespun faith and homegrown liturgical styles, the Celts began to think of themselves as spiritually superior to those in Rome. In the following verse, ostensibly written about the futility of going to Rome on pilgrimage, one senses the subtle criticism of Roman religious practice:

Who to Rome goes
Much labor, little profit knows;
For God, on earth though long you've sought him,
You'll miss at Rome unless you've brought him.

But for all its glory, the Celtic church was no match for the Roman hierarchy. In 664 at the monastery of Whitby on the northeastern coast of England, Roman and Celtic leaders had a showdown on two divisive issues: when believers should celebrate Easter and how monks should wear their hair.

The Celts, who did things their own way, arrived at their own calculation of the date of Easter. As a result, they celebrated this preeminent Christian holiday a week earlier than the rest of Christendom. To Rome's way of seeing things, the Celtic Easter tradition appeared to be the epitome of impudence. According to Bede, Pope Honorius wrote the Celtic believers, and "urgently warned them not to imagine that their little community, isolated at the uttermost ends of the earth, had a wisdom exceeding that of all churches ancient and modern throughout the world."

The hair issue was perhaps an illustration of Rome's discomfort with the Celts' open embrace of many pagan practices. Many religions require that their clergy have a distinctive shaven heard, or tonsure. The Roman tonsure involved shaving a circular patch on the top of the head, which was surrounded by a ring of hair. The Celtic believers copied instead the druids' tonsure, shaving the front half of their heads bald from ear to ear, and leaving long hair dangling from the back of their skull. After heated debate, a majority of the Celts caved in on both issues. Some renegades maintained their independent ways, but this resistance was short-lived.

Some historians conclude that Celtic Christianity really only flowered for a century and a half, following Patrick in the early sixth century to the Council of Whitby in 664. After Whitby, the pope's informal influence over the Irish church certainly became more official and authoritative, and gradually, the Celtic church began to lose its distinctive flavor. But Celtic Christianity flowered so magnificently that it still bears fruit today.

✤ A lasting influence

The Celtic church may have been destined to lose in its power struggle with its Roman brethren, much as the Celts' loose-knit tribal federations had early given way to the power of the Roman Empire. But the Irish missionaries won the hearts of the Celtic people. Even Bede, who disagreed with the Irish on just about every significant theological issue, agreed that the Celts lived out their faith in a commendable and compelling manner. Bede singled out St. Aidan, bishop of the island monastery of Iona, for special commendation, writing, "Among other evidences of holy life, he gave his clergy an inspiring example of self-discipline and continence, and the highest recommendation of his teaching to all was that he and his followers lived as they taught. . . . His life is in marked contrast to the apathy of our own times."

In addition, St. Cuthbert of Lindisfarne is remembered as an exemplary follower of Christ. The humble saint would have preferred to spend his life alone in communion with God, but because of the supernatural visions he received, he traveled far and wide to preach, hiking far up into remote mountain areas to spread the word. He allegedly treated everyone he met with the utmost courtesy and respect and won many to his way of thinking through little more than his example.

Pelagius: A Homegrown Heretic

In Celtic lands, paganism and Christianity intermingled for centuries. In the case of Pelagius, a British Celt born around 350, the Roman Catholic church decided that his mixing of the two doctrines resulted in heresy. His case gives us an interesting opportunity to examine the tensions between pagan pantheism and Christian theism.

One of the central conflicts over Pelagius's doctrine concerned the issue of free will. Pelagius taught that man was born with free will and argued that Christian adults could attain moral perfection. His disciple, Celestius, taught that infants were sinless from birth.

Augustine, who was one of Pelagius's most bitter adversaries, spoke for much of the Catholic church when he articulated a dimmer view. Augustine argued that the human will had been corrupted at the Fall of Adam and Eve, that humans were born sinful, and that all were in desperate need of God's saving grace.

The battle wouldn't have escalated if Pelagius had been a quiet, bookish theologian. Instead, he was a charismatic teacher and powerful writer. His treatise "On Nature," written around 414, convinced many to accept his views and inspired Augustine to write his rebuttal, "Nature and Grace," the next year.

A number of church synods met to issue an official determination on whether Pelagius was teaching the truth or lies. Two such synods held in Eastern cities failed to find anything wrong with his views. But Western synods held at Carthage and Milevis in 416 condemned him of heresy, and in 417 Pope Innocent excommunicated both Pelagius and Celestius.

Things didn't end there. A number of Catholic bishops refused to support Innocent's decision. In addition, the monk John Cassian, who had a powerful influence on the Celtic monastic movement, questioned Augustine's teaching about the utter sinfulness of human nature.

In 850, Irish-born theologian John Scotus Eriugena revived the debate. His famous work "On the Division of Nature" was condemned as pantheistic, and copies were ordered burned in 1225.

While Roman Christianity may have been unnecessarily skeptical about human nature, it's possible that Celtic Christianity was too upbeat. "While the ancient Celts certainly had a word for culpability or responsibility, they did not seem to have a clear concept of the Christian idea of sin," writes Peter Berresford Ellis in *The Druids*. Or as Andrew Greeley writes, "The thing about an Irish mystic or dreamer is that he can find God almost anywhere and runs the risk of encountering God everywhere."

The Pelagian conflict caused a huge stir in the early fifth century, and the episode remains one of the pivotal moments in the history of Christianity. However, the debate continues to the present, although in much different forms. One can find traces of Pelagian optimism today in everything from self-help groups, New Age beliefs, and even preaching that promotes the Christian faith as a pathway to health and wealth.

St. Brigid

Although she's one of the trilogy of key Celtic saints, we know much less about Brigid than we do about Saint Patrick. Part of this uncertainty is due to a lack of historical material, but another part of the problem is that Brigid's biography has been mixed with folklore, legend, myth, and miracle so that the real Brigid is lost in a cloud of confusing and often contradictory stories. Perhaps more than any other saint, Brigid's legend is intertwined with pagan myths and spiritual practices.

We know that she died sometime around 525. No one knows when she was born. Her feast day is celebrated on February 1, also the date of the pagan holiday of Imbolc, which celebrates the coming of spring after a long, cold winter. Her name is the name of a pagan goddess of fire and song.

In addition to her feast day and her name, we know the name of Brigid's famous monastery: Kildare, or "Church of the Oak." It's not clear whether the church was named after a nearby tree or whether there was some deeper association with a pagan shrine, but many believe Brigid Christianized an earlier pagan site, just as other monastery founders did.

The uniqueness of Brigid's monastery is also worth noting. Founded as a "double" monastery with facilities for both men and women, Kildare was a powerful symbol of the radical egalitarianism the Celtic Christians practiced. Regarded as one of the most important monasteries of the Celtic church, Kildare trained numerous monks and nuns, many of whom went on to found their own centers.

At Kildare, the devotion to God and to Brigid was so deep and strong that faithful members kept a fire burning in her honor there for more than a thousand years. The only thing that could put out that flame was the oppressiveness of the English regime, which shut down all of Ireland's monasteries following the Reformation.

It hasn't been so easy to extinguish the devotion the Irish people feel for this amazing saint. Today there are more monuments to Brigid and more churches named after her than there are for Patrick. In addition to the deep affection she inspires in her native Ireland, her name is affixed to a peak in the Himalayas, an island off Japan, and numerous locations in Scotland and England. Truly, this saint's powerful mythos has surrounded the globe. And back at home, she remains "the most celebrated Irishwoman of all time," writes Alice Curtayne.

▨ Finding and sharing your faith

The story of Patrick and the early Celtic Christians demonstrates that it's possible for just about everyone to find a faith that fits. These missionaries took the essentials of Christianity and expressed them in a new, exciting, and culturally relevant way. Their example can encourage us to reject one-size-fits-all religion and embrace God in a unique and personal way. Here are some ideas to help you think about ways to do that.

- **Find a group of believers you can belong to.** Spirituality isn't a solo sport. It takes community to grow closer to God. While many individuals don't find the sense of personal connection they need in large corporate worship settings, millions are finding a loving faith community in smaller groups that meet in each other's homes. In recent years, a "small group" movement has swept North America. Many churches encourage their members to gather regularly with eight to twelve other believers and talk together, pray together, and be open with one another. Such small-scale and personal forms of spiritual practice can help you apply truth to your life with greater effect.

- **Practice gracious evangelism.** Christianity and Islam are two of the more evangelistic faiths, and their adherents are taught to share the message of salvation with others. Whether you're a Christian, a Muslim, or a devotee of another faith, may I suggest that when you share your beliefs with others that you do so graciously? Nobody likes arrogance, and spiritual arrogance can be especially distasteful. Instead of proudly proclaiming that you're right and everybody else is wrong, why not try an approach that balances conviction with sensitivity and respect. Instead of hammering away at everyone you meet, consider looking for natural opportunities to share your beliefs.

- **Live out what you believe.** In reality, everyone is an evangelist. What kind of sermon are you preaching with your life? If people observe your actions without knowing your beliefs, what will they conclude about your deepest values and convictions? In the early 1200s, a humble man named Francis who hailed from the Italian town of Assisi told his followers, "Preach always. If necessary, use words." Centuries before Francis walked this earth, an energetic group of Celtic monks "lived as they taught." By that simple and profound act, they changed their world. The lives of the Celtic saints corresponded to the message they preached. That protected them from the sin of hypocrisy, and when they preached, it gave their words a ring of authenticity and truth.

7

MONKS AND MONASTERIES

A melodious bell, pealing out over the glen, such is the will of the fair Lord, that many brothers may be gathered under one discipline.

—"The Rule of the Grey Monks"

KEVIN WAS A GIFTED man born sometime in the fifth century to the royal line of the Dal-Mesincorb tribe. A skilled poet and acclaimed musician, he gave up all his worldly wealth and entitlements to follow the call of God, which to Kevin meant the call to live alone as a hermit in the wild. Ordained as a priest, Kevin didn't seek out a congregation or community he could shepherd. Instead, he fled to the wild expanses of Ireland's beautiful and stately Wicklow Mountains, and a lovely spot called Glendalough—which means "valley of two lakes."

A meditative mystic who practiced a harsh and rigorous life, Kevin slept little, ate less, and spent all the day in prayer. Legend has it that his small dwelling place was a cramped and uncomfortable cell carved into the side of a granite cliff. There, it is said, Kevin spent six months out of every year in somber shade. And there, in his own little world, Kevin prayed, meditated, talked to God, and communed with nature for seven solitary years. Though he is described as wearing only animal skins and sleeping on a bed of rocks, he experienced an otherworldly bliss in his solitary cell as "the branches and leaves of the trees sometimes sang sweet songs to him, and heavenly music alleviated the severity of his life."

Ironically, saints who flee the world to find God in solitude often attract a crowd. Call it one of the recurring patterns of the spiritual life of the species, but lone mystics become magnets for others who are seeking the same kind of intimacy with God. In Kevin's case, this solitary saint was soon surrounded by a handful of followers who wanted to learn from the holy hermit. In time the handful had turned into a few dozen. Within years, the dozens grew into hundreds. Soon, Glendalough was no longer the site for one man's solitude, but had evolved into the center of a large monastic community that housed monks, chapels, a school, and a farm. As would happen at other communities throughout the Celtic lands, Glendalough began to look more like a small, bustling town than it did a religious retreat.

The rhythms of the community's days were governed by Kevin's rule for his monks, which the saint wrote in verse. Unfortunately, Kevin's rule is now lost, as are the original buildings Kevin and his brothers built. But one can still see remains of some of the buildings that were used by monks and others in the centuries after Kevin's death in 618. The monastery flourished for another seven centuries, and monks still lived there until the sixteenth century, when the English government closed down all of Ireland's monasteries.

In addition to hundreds of monks, Glendalough also attracted thousands of pilgrims. The popularity of making pilgrimages to hallowed and holy sites has waxed and waned through the twenty centuries of Christian history, but pilgrimages have always been popular among the Irish. In time, Glendalough was one of Ireland's most visited Christian centers, and the site remains a powerful draw for pilgrims, tourists, and nature lovers today. Every year, hundreds of thousands of people visit Glendalough to look at its well-preserved monastic remains or stroll its lovely walking trails, which wind through the valley and alongside a lake.

The life of Kevin and that of his beloved Glendalough form a sort of pattern that would repeat itself during the fifth, sixth, and seventh centuries of Ireland's religious life. Like Kevin, holy men would flee the world. But before long, refugees from that world would huddle around the holy men, transforming their solitude into a vibrant new form of Christian community.

▨ A flowering monastic movement

Nobody knows for sure who started the first Celtic monastery. It's clear that a monastery grew in Patrick's center of Armagh, but this may have happened long after the saint's death. At least one writer claims the first Celtic monastic site was at Tintagel in southwest England, which may have been founded as early as 470. This beautiful windswept site, which is perched on the side of a steep Cornwall hill overlooking the pounding waves of the sea, is a stunning place with a number of ancient stone remains.

Of course, some of the earliest monastic settlements may have consisted of little more than a few believers huddled together in a cave or hut. If such small communities existed, and many think they did, any remains have long since vanished. Most scholars believe that the first Irish monastery was founded around 484 by Saint Enda on the rugged and rocky island of Inishmore, which is the largest of the three Aran Islands off the western coast of Ireland. Enda received the islands from Aengus, King of Cashel, and the saint established a small community that was known for its harsh rules, severe discipline, and total separation from the world.

Before Enda died around 535, his small community had become a beacon of monasticism for the rest of Ireland. At his school, Enda instructed numerous men and women who would later found their own Christian centers, including Brendan of Clonfert, Finian of Clonard, Jarlath of Tuam, and others. All his students praised Enda's exacting instruction, even if they didn't adhere to his strict rule.

Today there's not much left of Enda's original monastery. Shifting tides and drifting sands have washed away any remains of his original settlement. But the beautiful bay where he once prayed and taught is now a quiet and peaceful site that features the remains of a chapel built later, as well as dozens of Celtic-cross grave markers.

One of Enda's best-known disciples was Ciaran, who established one of the most renowned Celtic monasteries at Clonmacnoise. Ciaran was an unusual man who combined intense spiritual depth with an expansive evangelistic vision. Content to spend hours in mystic reveries, he also felt a passion for spreading the Christian message and the monastic lifestyle. These dual concerns led Ciaran to found Clonmacnoise at a busy crossroads in Ireland around 549. The site is on the banks of the River Shannon, Ireland's longest river, which was then a major north-south water route. The site is also on the border between two Celtic kingdoms, which meant Ciaran could draw support from both without being beholden to either. In addition, his chosen location straddled the island's most important east-west overland route: a roadway following the course of an ancient chariot path that ran along a natural ridge.

In a sense, all roads led to Clonmacnoise, and the monastery quickly became a bustling center of activity, even though its founder died of the yellow plague seven months after he established it. But those who came after Ciaran shared his vision for Clonmacnoise, and over the years kings prayed there, some of the world's best scholars taught there, and artists carved dozens of huge Celtic crosses there. Some of these magnificent crosses still stand among the site's impressive remains. The site, which is roughly midway between Dublin and Galway and due south of the present-day city of Athlone, is a popular tourist spot that allows guests to feel like they're stepping back into Ireland's distant past.

But Ciaran's Clonmacnoise is just one of the more celebrated of Ireland's monasteries. Many other brothers and sisters founded centers of their own, including Ita of Limerick, Finian of Moville, Comgall of Bangor, Brigid of Kildare, Mobi of Glasnevin, Brona of Clonbroney, and Maedoc of Ferns.

▩ Children of the desert fathers

Dysert O'Dea in Ireland's western County Clare is an ancient monastic site. It's named after one O'Dea, who refurbished one of the site's high crosses in the 1680s. But perhaps more puzzling is the first part of the name: *Dysert*, or *disert*, is an Irish word for "desert."

The mystery repeats itself throughout the Celtic world. There are Irish sites like Dysert in County Limerick, Dysart and Dysart Tola in County Westmeath, and Dysart Gallen and Dysartenos in County Leix, along with Dysserth (or Dyserth) in Wales, a spot that is often cool and moist. To understand why the term *desert* is associated with so many humid Celtic monastic sites, one needs to ignore climate and instead focus on the historic roots of Christian monasticism, a movement that was born in deserts of Egypt, Palestine, and Syria in the first few centuries after Christ. The movement actually began with hermits who fled to the desert to pray alone.

Antony of Egypt was among the first to organize these isolated hermits into groups, founding a number of communities near the Dead Sea in the early fourth century. Life in Antony's colonies was based on prayer, fasting, austerity, obedience, and battles with the Devil. His teaching centered on self-denial as a prerequisite to spiritual intimacy with God. Antony's "Life," written by Athanasius, helped the wider world get a taste of Antony's ideas.

Among those who studied Antony's "Life" and teachings were John Cassian and Martin of Tours, who spread his approach throughout Europe. It was probably at communities founded by these men that Celtic Christians were first introduced to Antony's teaching, and soon Celtic monks were creating their own deserts of

Cloicthech

When it came time to summon monks to prayer from the fields and from their labors in scriptoria and workshops, one of the monks would ascend the monastic round tower. The Irish word for these towers, of which there are more than sixty surviving today, was *cloicthech*, which meant "bell house" or "bell tower." In former times the ringing of the bell could be heard throughout the valley.

The round towers were much more than a convenient place to hang a bell, however. Built in the tenth century and after, and standing between seventy and one hundred feet in height, the towers made excellent lookouts, which came in handy as communities tried to protect themselves from Viking invaders.

In most round towers, the lowest opening was a doorway located ten feet off the ground. A wooden ladder was used to reach the doorway, then once the monks were inside the safety of the tower, they would take the ladder in with them.

There is also evidence that the towers were made to protect more than the monks. As Celtic monasteries grew in size and wealth, they accumulated possessions that would have attracted the attention of Viking raiders or even local bandits. The round towers often served as monastic vaults.

Although such raiders probably weren't scholars, they would often steal the monks' manuscripts, if for no other reason than to tear off their covers, which were often gilded with precious metals or embossed with valuable jewels. In addition, most large monasteries would have possessed Eucharistic goblets and instruments, intricately made bells, and other items that would have made nice booty.

In addition, round towers served as beacons for religious pilgrims who sometimes journeyed miles on foot to visit a monastery, receive a blessing from the monks, and touch the bones and holy relics from the monastery's earliest saints and founder. Some of the round towers could have been seen from miles away, and what a sight they would have been to weary pilgrims!

Interestingly, the round towers seem to be another uniquely Irish contribution to the Christian tradition. According to historian Peter Harbison, a former chairman of Ireland's National Monuments Advisory Council, there are only three examples of round towers outside of Ireland: two in Scotland and one on the Isle of Man. The sixty-plus examples still surviving in Ireland are in various states of preservation, but nearly all are missing the wooden stairs and floors that lined the inside of the towers. Some of these wooden materials have deteriorated over the centuries, others appear to have been burned by marauders.

One of the more interesting towers is the leaning tower at Kilmacduagh, County Galway, which is the Celtic equivalent of the leaning tower of Pisa, and excellent examples of round towers can still be seen today at Glendalough, Ardmore, Clonmacnoise, Devenish, and Kildare.

spiritual isolation among the rich and fertile Celtic lands. References to the so-called desert fathers pop up frequently in the writings of the Celtic saints. One early Welsh poem written in praise of the trinity mentions "the God of Paul and Anthony," a reference to two important Middle Eastern hermit/monks.

No one's sure why the monastic and ascetic practices that originated in harsh deserts had such an allure for the Celtic monks—much more so than they did in just about any other land. But one thing's clear: The monastic ideal became an important part of Celtic Christianity as it began growing, evolving, and eventually spreading over the face of the earth.

❧ Communal Christianity

Monasticism took off in Celtic cultures, and soon, monks and abbots (those who served as monastery directors) became the most influential religious figures in these previously pagan lands. In fact, as monastic settlements grew, operating schools and attracting a greater number of monks as well as "civilian" workers, monks began to take over many of the roles previously performed by the traditional druids and bards. The monastery's picture of the Christian life as a community affair was extremely attractive to the Celts, who placed a premium on the bonds of kin, clan, and tribe.

The new Christian communities, with their emphasis on the fellowship between Christian brothers and sisters under the fatherhood of God, were reinventing an ancient Celtic concept, and the Christian communities reaffirmed and reinterpreted many traditional Celtic values. Before the arrival of the Christian message, the pagan Celts felt themselves to be a part of a close-knit universe and believed they were surrounded by numerous gods, heroes, and ancestors. After Ireland converted, writes scholar Philip Sheldrake, there was "a new version of the old sacred universe now framed within Christian community structures. So the sacred place of the monastery took on the aspect of the clan enclosure and the abbot or abbess replaced the sacred ruler, or sometimes combined both roles." The Celtic monks who were adapting the work of desert monks like Antony created a new form of monasticism that was perfectly suited to their culture and warmly embraced by their people.

For years, Uinseann O'Maidin, a contemporary Cistercian monk who lives at Mount Melleray Abbey in County Waterford, has been collecting old Irish monastic rules and writings, some of which were translated into English in his fascinating 1996 collection, *The Celtic Monk*. These early documents describe the regulations governing the various monasteries, but they also give an idea of how joyous some of these spiritual settlements were. "The Rule of Cormac Mac Ciolionain" may be a typically upbeat example. "Happy the moment when I hear of a stable community, one not given to chatter," writes Cormac. "The melodious chant of the believers is as food to me. . . . The practice of confession, constant sorrow for sin, circumspection of behavior and fewness of words, all are characteristics of the monastic way of life. It is a wonderfully pure way of life not to be given to hateful lying."

Celtic Christians enthusiastically founded large numbers of monastic communities, which proliferated throughout Celtic lands and further accentuated the differences between these communal Christians and their more bureaucratic brethren in Rome. As one twentieth-century writer put it, the homespun holiness of the Celtic saints was worlds away from the Roman church's approach: "Celtic monks lived in conspicuous poverty; Roman monks lived well. Celtic monks were unworldly; Roman monks were worldly. Celtic bishops practiced humility; Roman bishops paraded pomp. Celtic bishops were ministers of their flocks; Roman monarchs were monarchs of their dioceses. Celtic clergymen said, 'Do as I do,' and hoped to be followed; Roman clergymen said, 'Do as I say,' and expected to be obeyed."

▦ A monk's life

Just as most of the monasteries built by the earliest Celtic monks have long ago crumbled and disappeared, many of the rules written to govern these communities have vanished from the face of the earth. We know that Brendan and Brigid, for example, wrote rules, but no trace of them can be found.

Such rules became necessary as monasteries proliferated and grew larger. A solitary hermit doesn't need a written rule. He can follow God as he sees fit and doesn't have to worry about conflicts with others. But once two or three hermits try to work together, misunderstandings can develop. And in a community of a dozen or more monks or nuns, confusion can reign if there's not a clear understanding of each individual's responsibilities to others and to the community as a whole. Most of the time, rules were written by a community founder and modified over the years by successive abbots or abbesses. Everyone who joined a community agreed to abide by its rule. Looking at the rules that have survived and have been translated by O'Maidin, it's possible to paint a picture of what life would have been like for a typical Celtic monk.

Many of the rules deal with the need for rules. To some, the whole business might sound like the worst form of repression, but to the thousands of Celtic monks, the laws that governed their lives meant liberty. Conformity to the rule meant freedom, or as one rule put it: "No one can captivate a person who willingly submits to the rule." It's impossible for any rule to cover every eventuality, and none of them were designed to.

But they did state—sometimes in dizzyingly broad strokes—the community's fundamental mission, and the individual members' primary responsibilities: "In this lies the heart of the rule: to love Christ, to shun wealth, to remain close to the heavenly king, and to be gentle towards all people."

Sometimes monastic rules stated members' obligations negatively: "Do not eat until you are hungry. Do not sleep until it is necessary. Do not speak until necessity demands." And sometimes they put things in the positive: "Each day carries with it three duties: prayer, work, and reading."

Prayer was a priority for all monasteries, and monks would spend time each day praying alone as well as praying with others. Most of the detailed regulations monasteries used were designed to make sure prayer didn't get squeezed out of the day by other more urgent but less important tasks. Physical labor was also an important part of the monastic day. Work was seen as inherently good, it provided necessary exercise, and it helped keep food on the table, even if in some monasteries food was eaten in tiny amounts. "Let each be given a loaf, thirty ounces in weight," ordered one rule, "with a twelve-inch cup."

Study was also seen as a beneficial pursuit, as long as it was used for the right ends. The Celtic monks were an especially studious lot, as we'll see in a later chapter. But even though studying about God could provide the monks with information about God, it couldn't give them spiritual intimacy with God. Thus, knowledge was valued most when it informed and guided members' often otherworldly mystical experiences. Study was designed to help monks grow closer to God, and if it became a hindrance or impinged on their prayer time, it was curtailed. When possible, study was combined with other tasks, such as eating, according to one rule: "The following is the custom. . . . One of them reads aloud the Gospels, the rules and the lives of the saints, while the rest are eating, that the minds of the monks may be centered on God rather than on the food." But neither eating nor talking was meant to detract from silent meditation: "There are three or four faults common to otherwise virtuous persons, such as being given to drawing others into endless chatter, and also addiction to delicacies."

Each monastery had "boundary" rules that were designed to insure the seclusion needed to practice spiritual discipline. At the most basic level, these boundaries urged a separation from the world: "Let your hermitage be a very secure place with only one door," one rule urged. But the physical separation was representative of a larger spiritual purpose. "If you have withdrawn from the world," one rule cautioned, "remember that you now walk a path of suffering. Do not look to the world, but rather flee from it as you would from a hue and cry." Another rule states: "Let your life be completely detached from the world, and follow the teaching of Christ and the gospels."

Every member of the community had his or her own role. "The Rule of Carthage," for example, detailed the responsibilities of each person, giving special attention to the duties of the abbot: "Preach diligently what Christ, the holy one, commands. . . . You should love the souls of all, just as you love your own . . . encourage the seniors . . . instruct the young. . . . Yours it is to reprimand the wayward, to correct all, to bring order to the disorderly, the stubborn, the willful, and the wretched."

Perhaps the best description of the monastic life is found in "The Alphabet of Devotion," which is believed to have been written by a monk in a monastery near Linsmore and provides a program of spiritual effort:

> Faith in good deeds, perseverance in desire, deligence with quietude, chastity with humility, fasting with moderation, poverty with largeheartedness, reserve in conversation, distribution with moderation, endurance but without hostility, abstinence without comparison [with others], zeal without discourtesy, meekness with truth, confidence without disdain, fear without contempt, poverty without pride, confession without self-vindication, teaching with fulfillment, advancement without retreat, humility in the face of pride, gentleness in the face of aggression, labor without grumbling, simplicity with prudence, obedience without favoritism, devotion without pretense—all of these go to make up holiness.

▨ From hermits' huts to monastic cities

From a distance, a Celtic monastery wouldn't have looked much different from the dirt and stone forts that dotted the land in earlier times. Most major monasteries were surrounded by large banks that enclosed the community, and depending on the time of day when you happened to visit, many of these monasteries would have resembled other nonreligious communities. In fact, when some of the larger monastic centers were going full throttle, they looked less like humble houses of prayer and more like small cities, complete with noisy workshops and forges, metalworkers and carpenters, and workers processing the harvests from the nearby fields.

At their peak, some communities were sunrise-to-sunset operations that had a thousand members or more. Only a small percentage of these people would have been monks, whose living quarters and worship areas were kept separate from the community's more secular concerns. In addition to the monks, the large circular monastic enclosures would have sheltered many additional residents, including students, workers, merchants, and various poor and homeless souls who had found comfort under the monks' care. At least one historian familiar with Celtic culture has asked whether these big, busy communities should even be called monasteries, since they were really so much more complex than that term usually implies.

As some of these communities grew, they became the largest settlements in all of rural Ireland. Over time, this meant that some of the monastic abbots wielded influence and authority over surrounding geographic regions. Some monks became influential social leaders who were responsible for the feeding, education, and medical care of increasingly large communities. Soon, they were advising kings and chieftains, brokering peace agreements between angry warlords, and writing laws. Ironically, the monks' once humble communities were beginning to look like smaller, scaled-down versions of the Romans' worldly centers.

All this success brought two unintended consequences. One was that some monks at some monasteries became so wrapped up in running their businesses and communities that they spent less time in prayer and meditation. When this happened, discipline and devotion declined, and many monasteries never regained the practice. Second, the growing wealth and affluence of the monastic communities made them prime targets for Viking raiders who made their first appearance along Ireland's coasts in the 790s. These raids would continue for the next two centuries, and by the year 1000 there were few monasteries that hadn't been attacked at least once.

Following centuries of internal decline and external pressure, many Celtic monasteries crumbled and closed. Others endured, but only with fresh infusions of energy and discipline from European monasteries, whose reforms swept across Ireland, removing the last traces of the monasteries' uniquely Celtic character. The final blows came in the sixteenth century, when Henry VIII of England began dissolving all the monasteries in England and Ireland and claiming their wealth for the crown, and later in the seventeenth century, when the ruthless Oliver Cromwell wiped out thousands of Irish, shipped thousands more off to places like Barbados as indentured servants, and rounded up in huge reservations those who remained.

But before these dark days, the Celtic monasteries burned bright with the light of devotion, helping to create a vibrant faith that spread across Europe. As nineteenth-century Irish poet Sean O'Coileain writes in his "Elegy

on the Ruins of Timoleague Abbey," "There was a time
when this house was cheerful and glad."

🎨 The legacy of the Celtic monks

Nearly all of the Celtic monasteries that began popping
up in Ireland fifteen hundred years ago are no more, but
we can still learn much from their tradition. Here are some
suggestions from the wisdom of the Celtic monks.

- **Find your own desert.** Many of us swim in a swift
stream of people, events, deadlines, and noise. Stress-
ful lives lead to early deaths for many, but even those
who survive the onslaught find the frantic pace of
modern life spiritually deadening. One antidote to the
chaos is to find a desert where you can enjoy the
seclusion and silence that are prerequisites for deep
spiritual growth. The Celtic monks created deserts of
splendid isolation throughout Ireland, Britain, and
Europe. Perhaps you can create—or find—a desert
refuge somewhere near you.

- **Visit a monastery.** Some monasteries are closed and
private communities. But the vast majority offer a variety of programs to the general public, such as training in prayer and mentoring in meditation. In
addition, many monasteries have hermitages where
people can find quiet and seclusion for a day or more.
Visit a monastery in your area and see how they can
help you along the way in your spiritual journey.

- **Form your own small community.** In today's busy
world, many people find personal caring and spiritual

depth in small groups that consist of church members and others who meet regularly in each other's homes. Many churches sponsor such groups, and see them as a necessary alternative to large and often impersonal worship services. I'm in a small group that's been meeting together, praying together, crying together, and eating together for five years. I would be a much smaller and lonelier person if it weren't for these wonderful brothers and sisters.

8

SILENCE AND SOLITUDE

Two thirds of piety consists of being silent.

—"The Rule of Ailbe"

THE MONKS WHO FOUNDED the remote and mysterious monastery at Skellig Michael wanted to make sure that their community would remain a quiet haven, where their meditations on God wouldn't be interrupted by the noise of the world. They wanted to be alone and otherworldly, not the center of one of the bustling new monastic cities that were springing up throughout Celtic lands. So when these single-minded monks chose a site for their monastery, they selected one of the most inaccessible, most inhospitable sites possible: a steep, rocky island eight miles out in the Atlantic off County Kerry's southwestern tip.

Wracked by winds and battered by waves that have gathered strength during their two-thousand-mile journey from the shores of Newfoundland, Skellig Michael sits where the Atlantic's Gulf Stream meets the rocky coast of Ireland. Because of unpredictable weather and the violence of the waves, the island can be completely inaccessible for days and weeks at a time. And that's just the way the monks wanted it.

If they were looking for silence and solitude, this was the perfect place. From the time monks first inhabited the island in the sixth century until they left in the twelfth century, Skellig Michael (the name is a combination of the Irish word for "rock" and the name of the archangel believed to bless high places) was a rugged sanctuary for a small community of about a dozen men, along with a few sheep and goats. (Cows and pigs would have fallen off the island's steep, rocky cliffs and right into the churning ocean below.) Ironically, the island's inhospitability and inaccessibility have helped protect the monastery's ancient remains, making Skellig Michael the world's best-preserved example of early Christian architecture.

Every year, between twelve and fifteen thousand pilgrims ride boats out to the island, where they can walk up some of the two thousand three hundred stone steps the monks lovingly created and that take visitors from the turbulence at ocean level to a calm, secluded monastic site nearly six hundred feet above the sea. The site, which has been carefully restored, features a half dozen stone "beehive" huts, all constructed without mortar by the monks, who spent years selecting and stacking the stones. In addition, there are two larger oratories, where the brothers would gather for prayer and worship. Regardless of whether one climbs onto the island or merely admires it from a safe distance, its stunning majesty and breathtaking beauty still strike visitors the way they impressed writer George Bernard Shaw, who said Skellig Michael possesses a "magic that takes you out, far out, of this time and this world."

While Skellig Michael does have forty-four acres of land, little of the island is level enough for gardens or crops, and researchers have concluded that the monks couldn't have grown enough food to sustain themselves. During much of the year, they would have dined on fish, birds, and bird's eggs, and they probably bartered their surpluses with mainlanders to acquire grain, firewood, and other necessities.

We don't know much about the monks who made their home on this rocky refuge. No written records have survived, which isn't particularly surprising. Beginning in the 820s, Viking raiders sacked the island, and they would continue to do so for centuries. Even if it weren't for human invaders, the harshness of the elements could have destroyed any vellum or parchment books the monks had created, much as the wind and waves have destroyed both a sturdy steel gate and a once sturdy lighthouse that were foolishly erected on the island.

🪷 Islands of calm

The monks of Skellig Michael may have been alone on their rocky refuge, but they were far from unique in seeking out remote locations for monasteries. If you look at the map of the British Isles, you can see that there are virtually no island monasteries on the island's eastern side—which faces England and Scotland—or its southern side—which faces mainland Europe. Such locations weren't considered secluded enough. Instead, there are numerous monasteries out in the ocean off Ireland's western coast, where there was nothing to bother the brothers but wind and waves. During the sixth and seventh centuries, monks established dozens of island monasteries throughout western Ireland.

Imagine Ireland as the face of a big clock, with Dublin representing three o'clock. Skellig Michael is located at about seven o'clock. North from there, at around nine o'clock, are a cluster of monastic outposts, including Enda's famous monastery on Inishmore, the largest of the Aran Islands, in Galway Bay. There are also sites on High Island and Inishbofin, roughly between nine and ten o'clock. At around ten o'clock is Inishmurray, located about midway between Sligo and Ballyshannon. At about eleven o'clock is Tory Island, northwest of Londonderry. And at one o'clock is Rathlin Island, off the coast near Ballycastle. In these remote island outposts, Celtic monks could pray to God with minimal diversions.

At the same time these religious refuges were established along the coast, other monks were fleeing to islands located in Ireland's many rivers and large lakes. Among the dozens of inland monasteries they settled, two are called Saint's Island and five named Church Island. Nor was it only in Ireland that monks fled to remote islands. Philip Sheldrake points to similar Celtic outposts off the coasts of Wales and Brittany. As Kenneth Hurlstone Jackson writes in *A Celtic Miscellany*, "The Celtic hermits went to the most desolate wilds and ocean rocks to win salvation in their own way."

Historians and archaeologists are grateful that the Celtic monks insisted on inhabiting these out-of-the-way sites, for their very remoteness has helped them survive through the centuries, providing a wealth of information for scholars and stunning sites for visitors. Their remoteness allowed these island monasteries to remain centers of devotion and contemplation, unlike mainland monasteries, many of which were rapidly becoming the hub of new Irish towns and villages. Although many monks may have visited places like St. Kevin's Glendalough, which had started out as one hermit's solitary refuge but evolved into a huge and influential monastic city visited by thousands of people, they didn't want their monasteries to follow a similar pattern. These island monks wanted quiet places to commune with God.

▨ Silence and solitude

What was it that drove these men and women to ever more remote and isolated enclaves? Simply put, such spots made it easier to focus on God free of the disturbing distractions of daily life.

Ours is a noisy, sensation-saturated world in which we are routinely bombarded with programmed entertainment or advertiser-sponsored messages during nearly every moment of our waking lives. Ride an elevator for fifteen seconds, and you'll be serenaded by Muzak's so-called soothing sounds. Call someone on the phone, and if you're put on hold, you'll hear bouncy background music or a come-on for a product you don't need or want. Even in rest rooms—which were once bastions of quiet and privacy—you are surrounded by canned music. In some restaurants, you can't even hear yourself think, for all the din. If you're fortunate enough to visit a park or nature site, you may find your quiet retreat interrupted by a blasting battery-powered boom box, or a rock concert–sized sound system stuffed into the back deck of a young person's car. In the average American home, the TV blares for more than six hours a day. And in between our noisy homes and our noisy workplaces, many of us fill the close confines of our automobiles with a cascade of sound waves, be it music, talk radio, or the latest book on tape.

Then there are all the unintentional noises that intrude on our sensitive souls. Trash trucks, lawn mowers, leaf blowers, vacuum cleaners, and hair dryers are just a few of the mechanized byproducts of our consumer culture. Their unannounced sonic assaults help make modern life more noisy.

Looking at this wailing wall of sound, some psychologists have wondered if all of us aren't addicted to noise, and some spiritual leaders ask if many of us aren't running from silence, afraid of what we might encounter there. Contrast our sound wave–saturated society with the quiet serenity of the Celtic monks, who ran to silence like it was a long-lost friend. They embraced the stillness, and instead of finding loneliness or emptiness there, they found God, along with a tremendous sense of inner peace and tranquillity.

Contrast your own noise-filled life with the serenity expressed by "Marbham's Hymn of Content," written by an Irish monk sometime during the tenth century:

> . . . I have a hut in the wood, no one knows it but my Lord; an ash tree this side, a hazel on the other, a great tree on a mound encloses it . . .

The size of my hut, small yet not small, a place of familiar paths . . .

A little hidden lowly hut, which owns the path-filled forest; will you go with me to see it? . . .

In summer with its pleasant, abundant mantle, with good-tasting savor, there are pignuts, wild marjoram, the cresses of the stream—green purity! . . .

The swarms of the bright-breasted ring-doves . . . the carol of the thrush, pleasant and familiar above my house . . .

Swarms of bees, beetles, soft music of the world, a gentle humming . . .

A nimble singer, the combative brown wren from the hazel bough . . .

Fair white birds come, cranes, seagulls, the sea sings to them, no mournful music . . .

A beautiful pine makes music to me, it is not hired; through Christ, I fare no worse at anytime than you do.

Though you delight in your own enjoyments, greater than all wealth, for my part I am grateful for what is given me from my dear Christ.

Without an hour of quarrel, without the noise of strife which disturbs you, grateful to the Prince who gives every good to me in my hut . . .

It's easy to picture the author of these peaceful words. You can sense his satisfaction in every line. Perhaps it's not surprising that a relatively large body of such poems was written in solitude, for it seems that Celtic Christians longed for a solitary hut in the woods just as much as we dream of a nice house in the suburbs.

The following lines are ascribed to Manchin Leith, who lived in the seventh century:

> I wish, O Son of the Living God, ancient eternal King, for a secret hut in the wilderness that it may be my dwelling. A very blue shallow well to be beside it, a clear pool for washing away sins through the grace of the Holy Spirit. A beautiful wood close by around it on every side, for the nurture of many-voiced birds, to shelter and hide in. Facing the south for warmth, a little stream across its enclosure, a choice ground with abundant bounties which would be good for every plant . . .

These monks and mystics exulted in the silence and solitude of their huts, but they didn't hide from themselves or their God. Instead, they turned a critical eye toward their own failings and faced their own mortality with a clear conscience. As one monk reflects: "All alone in my little hut without any human being in my company, dear has been the pilgrimage before going to meet death. . . . All alone in my little hut, all alone so, alone I came into the world, alone I shall go from it."

▦ Making space for God

Monks weren't antisocial introverts who were fleeing the world for their own personal comfort. They didn't flock to island monasteries and mountain hideaways because they esteemed people to be of little value. Instead, the Celtic monks put a premium on silence and solitude because they were trying to carve out a space for God in their lives. Seeing God as their ruler and a dear friend, these early Irish monks were trying to turn down the volume on all the noise and static of life so they could prepare a place for hearing the voice of God. Adomnan records in his "Life of St. Columba" that the saint's "dove-like life offered in himself a dwelling for the Holy Spirit."

In "The Life of St. Darerca, or Moninna, the Abbess," the biographer explains this holy woman's desire to leave her loved ones, study with the monk Ibar on one of Ireland's western islands, and start a convent of nuns. "She did not wish to have her devout intentions vitiated through empty discussions and inept conversations with lay people," the scribe writes, "or through frequent encounters with her parents." Explaining the lengths to which St. Darerca would go in order to better hear the voice of Jesus, the author notes: "She crossed over to a certain place situated on the slope of [a] mountain . . . so that there she could listen to the sweet discourses of her Spouse without any earthly impediment." As a result of her readiness, "as is proven to be true by the witness of those who knew her, angels often visited her and held familiar conversation with her."

As much as was possible, monastic rules spelled out detailed regulations to insure that their members could hear God above the communal din. "The Rule of Ailbe," which was probably written down sometime during the eighth century, devotes much attention to outlining how a monk could maintain a meditative quiet: "Let his work be silently done, without speech. Let him not be garrulous, but rather a man of few words. . . . Be silent and peaceful, that your devotion might be fruitful."

Frederick Buechner's novel *Godric* allows the modern reader to imagine what a typical day might have been like for a Celtic mystic. Even though the book describes the life of an English monk living in the eleventh and twelfth centuries, much of the material in this novel captures the activities, rituals, sounds, and smells that must have been common for Celtic monks of the sixth and seventh centuries as well. In one memorable passage, Buechner describes one of Godric's marathon prayer sessions with Ailred, a visiting mystic. As the author describes them, Ailred is "all bones. Godric's all rags. They kneel there for hours on end under the low thatch without a word to clutter the silence save for the prayers they heave heavenward."

▧ Combining contemplation and action

The four New Testament gospels are noisy. Matthew, Mark, Luke, and John are replete with stories full of action and talk: Jesus speaks to a crowd; he teaches as he travels with his disciples; he debates with the Jewish leaders in the synagogue; he is publicly hailed as the Messiah; and he is condemned to death in front of a large, angry mob.

Behind the scenes, however, Jesus was quiet and meditative. Frequently the gospels show him retreating from the crowds to speak with his heavenly father, to fast and pray in the desert for forty days, or to silently and urgently seek God's will before making important decisions or embarking on large public ministries. Likewise, the life of St. Patrick was full of both contemplation and action. His conversion to Christianity happened while he was utterly alone and tending sheep. As a slave in Ireland, Patrick began praying to God, and God met Patrick in his solitude.

In their desire to drink deeply from the wells of quiet and contemplation, the Celtic monks were reclaiming an important but much neglected aspect of Christian tradition. Like Jesus and Patrick, the seventh-century Celtic saint Cuthbert balanced bursts of energetic activity with lengthy periods of solitude and spiritual contemplation. And like Patrick, St. Cuthbert even had a vision while tending sheep. In his vision, Cuthbert saw a brilliant light illuminating hosts of angels who were ascending a long path to heaven.

After serving in various administrative positions at the monasteries of Ripon and Lindisfarne, Cuthbert—who is northern England's most popular saint—retired to the Inner Farne Island to be alone with God. Soon, however, Cuthbert attracted a throng of disciples who wanted to follow his example. Sensing that God was calling him to forsake solitude for a more public ministry, Cuthbert stepped back into the whirlwind. In 684 he was consecrated as a bishop, and soon he was the abbot of Lindisfarne. In addition, he was a tireless traveler and teacher who received a fair amount of acclaim for these public pursuits.

Even though he handled such duties with grace and efficiency, Cuthbert remained a mystic at heart, and he continually felt drawn to solitude and silence. As Bede tells us, Cuthbert would often express his desire to be away from the hubbub of high-profile work: "If I could live in a tiny dwelling on a rock in the ocean, surrounded by the swelling waves, cut off from the knowledge and the sight of all, I would still not be free from the cares of this fleeting world." Finally, after a period of activity and leadership, he again retreated to his beloved Farne, where he spent his final years in divine contemplation until his death in 687.

St. Fursey, one of the best known of the many Irish missionaries, was another seventh-century monk with a renowned public ministry and a heart for holiness. His preaching was legendary, and his travels took him over large parts of the globe. But as Bede tells us, "when Fursey had preached the word of God among the Irish for many years, he could no longer endure the crowds that thronged him. So he abandoned everything he seemed to possess . . . [and] freed himself of all worldly responsibilities and resolved to end his life as a hermit."

Fursey entered a period of solitude and silence, but this isn't the last we hear from him. He experienced a series of extremely vivid visions of the afterlife, which he recorded. In these visions, Fursey was able to see through the veils of this world and into the realm of good and evil spirits. He could also observe the experiences of people in the afterlife. His detailed, fantastic descriptions of the torments of hell and the bliss of heaven were studied and memorized by Christians for centuries, and Dante used them as one of his main sources when he wrote his epic *Divine Comedy*.

One could also name numerous other Celtic saints who supported their public work with the quiet foundation of contemplation. Findbarr was renowned for starting churches, as well as the monastery and city of Cork. The saint also spent a good deal of time as a hermit at Gougane Barra, a little island in a small mountain lake where there are still annual pilgrimages in the saint's honor. Colman, the abbot of Lindisfarne and the founder of the island monastery of Inishbofin off Ireland's western coast, spent a lengthy period in the mountainous and rocky Burren area of western Ireland, where he lived in the cleft of a rock with no company but that of a mouse. The rodent helped the saint in many ways, including waking him up for regular prayer.

But perhaps nobody practiced silence like the brothers encountered by Brendan, the sixth-century world traveler, during one of his fantastic voyages. Summoned by a bird and told to set sail, Brendan was sent to an island where he and his monks would spend Christmas with "four and twenty brothers." After finding the island and being welcomed by a "comely old man," Brendan and his men feasted and celebrated with the islanders—in total silence. As he was about to leave them and commence his journeys, Brendan asked how long the island monks had kept quiet. The elderly gentleman replied: "Our Lord knows no one of us has spoken to another these fourscore years."

🔲 Finding the balance

Before he became known as the founder of the monastery at Glendalough, Kevin was a solitary hermit who spent seven years alone in the wilds of the Wicklow Mountains. A beautiful legend from this period of his life illustrates the commitment and devotion of the Celtic monks.

There's a prayer that many of the monks practiced called the cross vigil. During the vigil, the worshipper would stand or kneel in prayer and extend his arms out from his body, much as Christ's arms were extended when he was crucified. The object of the prayer was to keep the arms outstretched for an unbelievably long period of time, past the point when the pain became unbearable. Monks saw the cross vigil as a way to experience a portion of the pain Christ endured on the cross.

Legend has it that Kevin practiced the cross vigil with such single-minded devotion that a blackbird from a nearby tree came and built a nest in his hands, laid a clutch of eggs in the nest, and roosted until baby birds were born. Through it all, Kevin kept at his prayers, so rapt in devotion that he either failed to notice what the bird was doing or refused to let it deter him from his prayers.

For true believers, this legend is a powerful symbol of the spiritual depth and vitality of Celtic Christianity. For others, it's a potent symbol of the alleged excesses of the Celtic monks. For example, St. Mochuda criticized St. Cronan for establishing a monastery in such an out-of-the-way location that it was virtually impossible for normal people to reach it: "To a man who avoids guests and builds his church in a wild bog, away from the level road, I will not go; but let him have beasts of the wilderness for his guests."

Leaders of the Roman church looked with derision upon the more extreme behavior of some of the wild

Celtic monks. Church leaders even discussed ways they could curtail such activities, but ultimately they didn't have to, as history took its course, and a number of factors led to the decline of the monasteries. One was Viking raids, which began in the 790s and destroyed many monasteries, plundering their goods, killing their monks, and laying waste to priceless libraries in order to steal metal and jewels off the luxurious book covers. But even before the Vikings arrived on the scene, some of the monasteries experienced decline and lack of discipline when their pioneering founders died and were replaced by less visionary abbots. Other communities were so mystical and otherworldly that their members gave insufficient attention to institutional survival, and the communities died off or vanished from the scene.

Some critics would charge that Celtic monasticism declined because it was spiritually unbalanced. Compare the Celtic monks to the followers of St. Francis, for example. St. Francis wanted his friaries to be far enough away from the hubbub of cities to protect the members' solitude, but close enough to the people to be of service to them. Seen next to such Franciscan communities, many Celtic monasteries seem to have been too otherworldly to be of any worldly good.

Still, during the sixth and seventh centuries, when the Celtic monastic movement flourished, it did accomplish a number of amazing things. First, it helped nurture a unique and mystical Christian expression that had a strong appeal among the pagan Celtic people. Second, it trained and educated many evangelist monks who re-Christianized Europe by taking the Christian message to these barbarian-dominated lands. And finally, the monks' commitment to study played a part in the preservation of some of the most important literary works in Western civilization, as we'll see in later chapters. Before we close this chapter, however, it should be said that critics of the Celtic monks' excesses seem to be outnumbered by those who think these often wild and woolly believers had precisely the spiritual energy and depth necessary to allow the Celtic church to survive some extremely difficult times.

🔲 Searching for solitude

You may not want to cross the ocean in search of a remote island where you can pray and meditate. But you've probably had moments when you felt that your life was spinning out of control and that a brief period of solitude would help you regain your balance. If so, you're not alone. Many people are looking for ways to quiet down their noisy lives. Here are some suggestions.

- **Fast from entertainment.** Many of us use television, music, and other entertainments to fill in the quiet, lonely places in our lives. Instead of flicking on the TV as soon as you get home, why not spend a few moments in silence. Or, if you live in a noisy neighborhood or apartment building and can't get a moment's peace, how about putting a compact disc of Gregorian chant or calming classical music on the stereo instead of the fast-paced, high-energy stuff that typically fills the airwaves. Either way, focus on turning down the volume in your life instead of always adding more noise and nonsense.

- **Take a personal retreat.** Not everyone is cut out to be a monk, but everyone needs times of silence and solitude. One practice many people follow is to schedule regular private retreats at a monastery or other spiritual center. There, away from the phone, the usual pressures, and the typical interruptions, you can spend some time alone with yourself and with God. People who do this regularly claim it quiets their souls, clears out their minds, and calms their hearts. And many say they get a clearer vision of their purpose in life by taking periodic breaks from the busyness.

9

CONTINUAL PRAYER

Only a fool would fail
To praise God in His might
When the tiny mindless birds
Praise Him in their flight.

—Sixteenth-century prayer

PRAYER CAN MEAN DIFFERENT things to different people. For some, it's of little importance. For others, it's a lifeline to God. Prayer can conjure up images of remote rituals, where the point is lost in a drone of "Thee's" and "Thou's." To many, prayer is the spontaneous reaction to fear or uncertainty. A struggling single mother who receives an unexpected bill in the mail might respond by sighing, "Dear God, how am I going to make ends meet?," while the most popular prayer is surely the urgent plea—for strength, comfort, even life—in dire circumstances. As the saying goes, "There are no atheists in foxholes." Celtic Christians often lived at the mercy of the elements or in fear of attack from a nearby tribe or distant Viking raiders, but such desperate prayers would hardly have exhausted the repertoire of requests and reminders they nearly continually sent up to God.

For the Christian Celts, prayer was a way of life, an umbilical cord to their heavenly creator and sustainer. In times of danger, they asked God for help; and in times of happiness, they thanked God for blessings. During the vast majority of times that were neither dark with fear nor light with bliss, prayer was part of their ongoing relationship with God. Their prayers were both mystical and natural, subconscious and deeply felt, reverential and conversational. Prayer was an ongoing dialogue, something like the easy exchange of words that passes between friends and lovers.

Celtic culture had always exhibited a strong tendency toward mysticism. Celts had a deep belief in the immanence of the gods and goddesses. Their landscape was dotted with reminders of the presence of otherworldly beings. Daily rituals, as well as special celebrations, were designed to express this awareness of the closeness of the divine.

When St. Patrick came to Ireland in the fifth century, and when Christian beliefs mixed with the Celts' pagan practices, the Christian evangelists didn't so much change the way people believed, but rather they redirected their devotion. Instead of praying or performing rituals to hundreds of localized gods and goddesses, people now prayed to a God who was both vast and personal, both powerful and compassionate. Many Celtic Christians described their intimacy with God in the same terms they might use to describe sexual intimacy with a spouse.

Although their approach might seem unusual to someone reared on a less vibrant manner of worship, the Celtic way of prayer can give us some practical methods for deepening our prayer life today.

⛤ Columba on prayer

St. Columba, also known as Columcille, is one of the towering figures in the flowering of Celtic Christianity. Born to a noble family line in 521, Columba is known for his important contributions to numerous facets of Celtic Christianity, including monasticism (he founded Iona and other centers), evangelism (many of his disciples were key figures in the re-Christianization of Europe), and learning (he wrote numerous poems and sermons, and Iona is believed to be the site where work on the famous Book of Kells was started).

Perhaps less well known is Columba's theology of prayer. His contributions on this topic are both deeply metaphysical and extremely concrete and can help us develop an approach to prayer that is both personal and practical. Among this compelling saint's numerous surviving writings is a sermon that spells out some of his views on mysticism and prayer. Quoting from the New Testament Gospels, Columba cites Jesus' invitation to his followers: "Let him who is thirsty come to me and drink." As Columba explains this metaphor, "Thus the Lord himself, our God Jesus Christ, is the fountain of life, and so he calls us to himself, the fountain, that we may drink of him."

Clearly, Columba sees Christianity as more than a mere creed, but also as a living, vibrant relationship with God; and he sees Christ as more than a good teacher and exemplary man, but also as a living presence who can visit us and bring us refreshment when we are spiritually thirsty. In his discussion of personal mysticism, Columba uses the language of erotic love to describe spiritual rapture. "Let us always drink of him with a fullness of longing," he writes, "and let the sweet savor of his loveliness ravish us." Columba describes the deep longing for communion with Christ as a prerequisite for true intimacy with God in his prayer:

> . . . We ask nothing other than that you should be given to us; for you are our all, our life, our light, our salvation, our food, our drink, our God. I ask that you inspire our hearts, our Jesus, with that breath of your Spirit, and wound our souls with your love. . . . Blessed is such a soul which is thus wounded by love.

In addition to his own words, we have numerous descriptions others wrote about Columba's practice of prayer. Adomnan's "Life of St. Columba" recounts the "angelic apparitions that were revealed to others about the saint, and to him about others." Included in his biography is a story entitled, "How a great number of holy angels were seen, coming down from heaven to confer with St. Columba." In the story, Columba addresses his brothers of Iona, telling them that he is going away to the western coast of the island to pray and requesting that no one accompany him. But one curious monk couldn't resist the urge to follow the holy father at a distance, and he situated himself on a hill that overlooked the spot where Columba was praying. From there, according to the story, the brother "could see St. Columba standing on a knoll among the fields and praying with his arms spread out towards heaven and his eyes gazing upwards." As the brother watched, he saw that "holy angels, the citizens of the heavenly kingdom, were flying down with amazing speed, dressed in white robes, and began to gather around the holy man as he prayed." In another collection of stories about the saint, Lady Gregory records that some of Iona's brothers entered a chapel where Columba was praying and saw the room full of angels communing with and ministering to the saint.

Modern skeptics may view such stories as the religious enthusiasm of a very dark age. Others may interpret the stories metaphorically, concluding that scribes and priests were trying to describe Columba as a holy man, and this was the way they chose to do so. But one won't understand much about the heart of Celtic Christian spirituality by demythologizing such legends, for the Christian Celts believed strongly in two things: first, the existence of a personal God, angels, and other spiritual entities; and second, that they could have regular communication with these spiritual beings.

🔲 Powerful prayers

It may seem unwise to use Columba as an example of the practice of prayer. "He's a saint, after all," some may say. "What does that have to do with me?" But instead of focusing on the prayer lives of saints, we can turn our attention to the prayer lives of ordinary people. Many of their common prayers, which have been collected in the past hundred years by researchers, have been handed down to us, possibly through centuries.

Many of these books are based upon the work of the most famous collector of all: Scotland's Alexander Carmichael. Born in 1832 to a farming family on the island of Linsmore, Carmichael worked as a civil servant, which gave him plentiful opportunities to visit Britain's Western Isles, also known as the Outer Hebrides. During his travels, he struck up acquaintances with the local folk, visited them in their homes and on their farms, and wrote down thousands of their prayers and blessings, collected in his *Carmina Gadelica* published in six volumes between 1900 and 1961.

Carmichael published the prayers in their original Gaelic as well as his own King James–style English translations. Those collections have been used by numerous others, including G.R.D. McLean, whose *Poems of the Western Highlanders* first appeared in 1961, and Esther de Waal, a contemporary British author of numerous works, including *The Celtic Vision* and *The Celtic Way of Prayer*.

🪷 Praying with the Celts

More recently, Uinseann O'Maidin, a Cistercian monk and archivist at Mount Melleray Abbey, a large, stately monastery situated on a majestic ridge overlooking the countryside around Cappoquin, an hour west of Waterford, has collected and translated a number of traditional Irish prayers. Although it's impossible to assign a firm date to these prayers, he believes many are two to three hundred years old, and were spread throughout Ireland by wandering bards and priests.

Many of the prayers were said at mealtime, which then as now was a popular moment for people to gather together, pause for reflection, and thank God for the blessings of life. One brief prayer, as simple as it is timeless, seeks to sacramentalize one of the most basic and important human functions: "O Virgin Mary and Son of God, bless this food, bless this drink." Few Celtic prayers are so simple, however. Many move from such practical matters as thanks given over a meal to other wide-ranging spiritual and theological concerns. As you read over the following prayers, you might think about finding creative ways to make them your own, adapting them to your personal needs and concerns.

A glimpse of eternity—In their humble desire to thank God for the blessings of life, many Celtic Christians expanded the time frame of their prayers. Instead of merely thanking God for the meal before them now, they also expressed thanks for previous meals:

Glory, praise, and thanks to you, O God, for this food and our good health.

We also thank you for all the food and health for which we have not thanked you.

Another prayer sends "Praise and glory to God for all the food he has ever given us."

The following prayer expresses a confident trust in the ongoing blessings of God and gives thanks for meals yet to come:

May the most generous Lord be praised, may he always be praised.

Praise and thanksgiving to Jesus for what we have eaten and will in the future eat.

Extending its frame of reference even further, the following blessing invokes God's continuing support beyond the boundaries of time:

All praise to the King of heaven, all praise be yours O God, all praise to Jesus Christ for this meal. He has granted us this food on earth; may he also grant us eternal food in heaven.

And another prayer uses the occasion of a meal to thank God for spiritual sustenance as well:

May he who has given us this food, grant us eternal life to our souls and to the souls of the seven generations who have gone before us.

These five simple prayers demonstrate in a powerful way how the overflowing faith of these Celtic people enabled them to see simple mealtime blessings as the opportunities to thank God for much more than today's food and drink. Perhaps they can help you broaden and enrich your own mealtime prayers.

Seeing the eternal in the temporal—As we have seen already, Celtic Christians had a unique ability to see beyond the temporal facts of life to the realities of eternity. This broadened perspective made even the simplest prayers windows to a much bigger reality. In the following prayer, which may have been said by believers before they were about to receive the gifts of the Mass, virtually nothing was mundane:

> May God bless us. May he bless us. Bless us O Lord, and these your gifts which we are about to receive through Christ our Lord. May it be the Lord's will to bless us. May the King of eternal glory grant us our share in the heavenly banquet.

The specific occasion of the following prayer has been lost. All we have is the heartfelt desire to look beyond the constraints of space and time:

> May we have the vision of heaven;
> May we hear the glory of the saints.
> Lord grant us your grace,
> together with patience and repentance
> and may you preserve us on the path of
> righteousness.

Prayers of protection—Human life is fragile, and the dangers surrounding us are many. The Celtic Christians understood this and made requests to God for protection a regular part of their prayers. The three prayers that follow express the normal concerns and fears of daily life, but do so with a calm reassurance that springs from a deep trust in a gracious heavenly father. This first prayer asks for the protection of God's angels:

> Take me under your protection O beloved angel of God, just as the Lord of grace so ordained. Accompany me at all times and protect me from worry and danger.

The Celts lived in turbulent times, and they had an awareness that death could strike them at any time. They wove this concern into their entreaties:

> I place my soul under your protection O Lord; save me from sudden death. Praise and thanks be yours forever.

Less urgent but no less sincere was this prayer, which was said before retiring to bed:

> O Glorious Virgin Mary, take me and my cares under your protection until morning.

Prayers like these were never uttered with the certainty that no harm would befall the one making the request. But in the very act of saying such prayers, the Celts experienced the peace that comes from knowing that their burdens didn't need to be borne alone. Now, part of the responsibility for the worries and anxieties of daily life was under the benevolent care of a loving God.

Luxuriant praise—Celtic believers understood that God was not merely the source of gifts and favors, and this awareness permeated their prayer life, which included numerous expressions of thanks and praise. The following prayer, recorded in County Donegal, attempts to enumerate God's blessings:

> A thousand thanks to you, O King of the
>   universe;
> a thousand thanks to you, O Lord of grace,
> for what you have given since our birth,
> and for what you will give us until the day of
>   our death.

This prayer, recorded in County Kerry, where the beauty of nature gives residents many a "fine day," mixes thanks with additional requests and ups the ante in enumerating God's blessings:

> We give a hundred thousand thanks to you, great, all-powerful God, who have given us these gifts. May Jesus and the glorious God of heaven protect us against him who would harm us in health of soul or body. May he who gave this food

for the body grant us a fine day, a life without shame or dishonor . . . a good death and in heaven the eternal food of our soul.

This prayer from County Galway is even more effusive in expressing thanks:

I give a thousand and a thousand million thanks to your merciful power, who have given us on earth this food. Grant eternal life and glory to our souls.

Prayers of submission to God—One of the most powerful prayers of the New Testament comes from the darkest moment of Jesus' life. As he was dying on the cross, Jesus looked to heaven and sighed, "Not my will but yours be done." This brief and spontaneous outburst of submission to the will of God has inspired believers throughout the centuries, including the Christian Celts, who in addition to telling God what they needed, let God know that they would give what He needed as well.

This prayer adds an element of submission to an otherwise straightforward mealtime prayer:

Bless O Lord, this food which we are about to eat for our bodily welfare.

May we be strengthened thereby to do your holy will.

Another mealtime prayer expands on this theme:

We give you thanks, Lord God, for this food. In your mercy grant that we may spend our lives, health, and strength for your glory.

There are numerous Celtic prayers that ask for nothing but God's guidance and request nothing but a stronger desire to submit to the divine will:

Purify my heart daily O Lord Jesus; make my will subject to the all-powerful sway of your love. Always direct my life Lord God, and let my thoughts and words be always pure.

And sometimes these prayers of submission asked for God's help to prevent those praying from disobeying his will:

May God grant that we never say or do anything harmful to ourselves or to our neighbors.

In the following mealtime prayer, thanks is mixed with the expression of willingness to take specific action to fulfil God's will for the poor and the oppressed:

Bless, O Lord, this food which we are about to eat. May it benefit us in body and soul. Should there be any poor creature who is hungry or thirsty passing by our house, send him in to us that we may share our food with him, just as God shares his blessings with us.

This prayer from County Waterford asks for God's granting a deeper spiritual connection:

> O Jesus meek and humble of heart
> make my heart as yours is.
> O heart of Jesus
> may I always have a great love of you.
> O heart of Jesus on fire with love of us,
> inflame our hearts with love of you.

Perhaps this brief, simple prayer may catch the attitude of submission best of all:

> O God, all powerful, you are my strength.

> O Lord of the world, my life is yours.

The ultimate act of submission may come at death, as it did with Jesus. The following prayer expresses the faith of one who can wholly put his life in God's hands:

> O Jesus, son of David, you have given us to see the light of day.

> May you carry us home with you to the city of grace.

🔲 Praying to the Creator

There's another important aspect of Celtic prayer that we can recognize today, which is the acknowledgment of God as creator and sustainer of the cosmos. The Celts were close to the earth, and at nearly every moment they saw a fresh opportunity to praise the Creator. Today, the only nature many people see is a potted plant in a window, or a weed growing in a crack between two slabs of concrete. Perhaps the Celts' effusive nature prayers can help us reorient our vision and encourage our hearts to praise God more.

Celtic Christians often mixed prayers for protection and guidance with deep thanks to God for the beauty of nature. O'Maidin's collection, *The Celtic Monk*, includes the following prayer "To God the Father":

Have mercy on us O God, Father almighty.
O God of hosts.
O noble God.
O Lord of the world.
O unutterable God.
O Creator of the elements . . .
O God of the earth.
O God of fire.
O God of the waters of wonder.
O God of the gusting and blustering air . . .
O God of the waves from the depth of the ocean.
O God of the planets and the many bright stars.
O God, creator of the universe and inaugurator of night and day . . .

Another prayer to the Creator brings together visions of heavenly glory and images of the beauty of the physical world praising "The maker of all things,/The Lord God worship we:/Heaven white with angel's wings,/Earth and the white-waved sea." The prayer "Christ's Bounty" opens with a plea for forgiveness, then moves on to praise God for nature's beneficence:

> You make the bright sun bless my head,
> Put ice beneath my feet,
> Send salmon swarming in the tides,
> Give crops of wheat . . .
> You crowd the rivers with fine fish,
> The sky with birds . . .
> You make the small flowers thrive
> In wholesome air,
> You spread sweetness through the world.
> What miracles can compare?

None of the Celtic saints expressed the love of nature so clearly as St. Columba. Perhaps, then, it's no accident that Columba chose an island setting for his monastery of Iona. Not only did the site provide seclusion for the community, but it gave the brothers a front-row seat to observe the beauties of nature and the majesty of the sea. The following poem is attributed to the beloved saint:

> I long to be in the heart of an island,
> on a rocky peak, to look out often upon
> the smooth surface of the sea.

To see the great waves on glittering
ocean ceaselessly chanting music to
their Father.

The Christian Celts didn't only pray about nature,
they prayed in nature. They surrounded themselves with
the beauty of creation, and the spontaneous response
of their hearts was to bless the Creator who was responsible for it all.

✠ pray always, and in all ways

In his first letter to the Thessalonians, the Apostle
Paul gave this advice: "Be joyful always; pray continually; give thanks in all circumstances." Perhaps more
than any other people, the Celts took Paul at his word.
Once, a monk approached St. Samthann and asked her
about the best way to pray. The monk wondered if he
should pray sitting, standing, or lying down. The saint's
response was direct: "In every position, a person should
pray." The Celts prayed nearly always and communi-
cated with God in nearly all ways.

Celtic monks, in particular, made prayer a continual
act. "The Rule of Ailbe" says the good monk "should be
constant in prayer. . . . Be faithful to prayer in your cell,
not troubling yourself with outside affairs." "The Rule
of Comghall" also encouraged constancy: "A fire built of
fern soon dies out. Do not be like flotsam, going with
every current, if you wish to persevere in devotion."
"The Rule of Columcille" (or Columba) told monks to
pray for others. "Pray constantly for those who annoy

you," it urged. "Be very constant in your prayers for the faithful departed, as if each dead person were a personal friend of yours." Elsewhere, Columcille's rule says monks should pray until it hurts: "The extent of your prayer should be until tears come."

Even though Celtic monasteries emphasized constant prayer, they balanced that emphasis with the realization that doing any one thing for long hours on end leads to delusion, not devotion. One of the monastic rules sought to avoid this error: "Do not practice long-drawn-out devotions, but rather give yourself to prayer at intervals, as you would to food. Pious humbug is an invention of the devil."

Nonetheless, the Celtic monks remained aware of their obligations. "What a trial it is to go to vigils as the wind burns my ears," wrote one monk. "Were it not for the fear of the Lord I would ignore the bell, sweet sounding though it be."

🔹 Just do it

Reading about prayer is similar to taking a driver's license exam. In either case, the goal is to finish the preparation and get out on the road where things are really happening. Here are a few suggestions for applying the Celts' wisdom to your own prayer life.

Asceticism: Praying Until It Hurts

Asceticism, the practice of renouncing physical pleasures or inflicting physical pain as a means of achieving spiritual enlightenment, appears at the devout end of most major world religions. Celtic Christianity, Uinseann O'Maidin points out, was "ascetic in the extreme."

The Celtic Monk, O'Maidin's collection of early monastic writings and rules, provides a record of the monks' harsh spiritual diet. "Let him make a hundred genuflections before the *Beati* in the morning, prior to his reading," says "The Rule of Ailbe." "In the evening he should again make a hundred genuflections." Elsewhere, the same rule described monks as worshipping God "with an abundance of tears flowing from emaciated cheeks."

Other rules were even more strict. "The Rule of Comghall" called for monks to practice two hundred prostrations, and during Lent one was to self-administer "two hundred strokes of the rod on the hand." Fasting was common, with some monks eating so little that they left themselves weakened and their health damaged. "The monk should be given to bodily penance even to the extent of [having] a miserable and emaciated frame," says "The Rule of Cormac Mac Ciolionain."

"The Rule of Tallaght" instructed monks to practice "self-flagellation from . . . Easter to Pentecost," as well as "self-castigation," adding verbal assaults to physical ones.

Many monks practiced asceticism while they slept. Most only slept a few hours, but many followed Columba's example, using a bare rock slab for a bed and a stone for a pillow.

Novelist Frederick Buechner captures this harsh asceticism in his Pulitzer Prize–nominated novel, *Godric*, which is a fictional treatment of a very real saint who reportedly lived in England from around 1065 to 1170. One passage describes not only Godric's self-inflicted punishments, but his spiritual motivation for doing so:

> Like Jacob's, my pillow is a stone, and when I raise myself to prop my back on it, my iron vest nips deep into my flesh. The nip's to chasten me and keep me mindful of the crueler nips our Savior bore for us upon the cross. . . .

Elsewhere, Godric describes his renunciations as gifts given to God: "The fire that I didn't build for heat, the wool for warmth I went without, the food I didn't eat—all these were like the trinkets that a man gives to a maid."

Before founding his monastery at Bangor, St. Comghall lived as a hermit on an island in Lough Erne, County Fermanagh. Soon he was joined by disciples who wanted to follow in his footsteps, but Comghall's rule was so harsh that seven of them reportedly died of cold and hunger. Before his death, Comghall suffered from a number of debilitating diseases, and some monks viewed these ailments as a divine judgment from God for Comghall's excessive harshness with himself and others.

In fact many Celtic monks were critical of the excessive asceticism of Comghall and others, and they called for balance and moderation. "The Alphabet of Devotion" calls for "temperate zeal," and "The Rule of Tallaght" points out the consequences of a monk who practiced seven hundred genuflections every day: ". . . His legs became so stiff that he was unable to make even a single genuflection as a result of the excessive number he formerly made."

- **Give thanks always.** At mealtime, at bedtime, and at just about any time of the day, the Celts gave thanks to God for the blessings of life. Have you given thanks to God lately? If not, make a list of people and things you're glad are in your life. Or try walking around your house as you express your gratitude to God for so many marvelous gifts. You may want to create your own prayer. Don't be thankless. Instead, give thanks to God.

- **Look for the divine in the daily grind.** No matter what they were doing, the Celtic Christians could find there a window to the divine. Mealtime was a chance to give thanks for food and request God's guidance in life. The beauty of nature inspired people to praise God for creating the universe. Try to look at things from this divine perspective as you're driving through town or walking across your office. Pray for the people you pass and the needs you see, and as you're praying, ask God to guide your life.

- **Pray your own way.** One day, Jesus left behind the crowds, gathered his disciples around him, and began teaching them about the kingdom of heaven. This lesson, now called "the Sermon on the Mount," contained instruction on how to give praise. "This, then, is how you should pray," said Jesus, before giving his followers the first rendition of something we now call "The Lord's Prayer." Probably the world's best-known prayer, this excellent example of how to pray can be found in the sixth chapter of Matthew. You may also find helpful examples in the Celtic prayers included in this chapter, or collected in other books.

  At the same time, make sure that you pray your own way. It's all right to learn from others, but for prayer to be most effective it has to come straight from your heart. Learn to pray in a way that is natural for you, sharing your concerns, feelings, and fears with God in a manner that's transparent and real. Don't fill your prayers with flowery-sounding language that blocks your conversation with God. Instead, talk to your creator as you would a close, trusted friend.

- **Give of yourself.** Consider giving something to God instead of making a request for something to be given to you. Go to God with open hands, submitting your life and your will to the care of the one who looks after all of creation.

10

WANDERING FOR GOD

Shall I leave the prints of my knees on the sandy beach, a record of my final prayer in my native land?

—Prayer of St. Brendan

THE *NAVIGATIO SANCTI BRENDANI ABBATIS*, also known as *The Voyage of Saint Brendan* is a fantastical tale of the travel and transformation on the high seas by one of the most famous of Celtic saints. The challenge comes when one tries to separate history from hagiography, fact from fantasy, and mysticism from maritime adventure.

We know that St. Brendan actually lived, but few details of his life are certain. He was born sometime around 486 in western Ireland's beautiful County Kerry. He founded many Christian centers, including Clonfert, which quickly became one of Ireland's major monastic schools. He died in 578. But there's no conclusive evidence to support some of the most elaborate claims about the saint: that he and his men sailed the oceans for seven years in search of a promised paradise, that he visited Iceland and North America, or that he battled huge sea monsters. On the other hand, such things can't be ruled out, either.

Legend tells us that Brendan heard a sermon based on one of the more enigmatic teachings of Jesus. According to Matthew 19:29, Christ said that "everyone who has left houses or brothers or sisters or father or mother or children or fields for my sake will receive a hundred times as much and will inherit eternal life." Brendan took the sermon to heart and prayed to God for permission to cross the seas in search of the so-called Land of Promise, an Edenic paradise believed to be located in the sea to the west of Ireland's rocky western coast. Soon, an angel appeared to Brendan, saying, "Arise, Brendan, that which thou hast requested thou shall receive of God, and that is to visit the Land of Promise at last." What followed was a series of adventures and misadventures that required two separate voyages and seven years. A cross between the New Testament Gospels and Homer's *Odyssey, The Voyage of Saint Brendan* is a big, bold tale of spiritual quest writ large over a background of surf.

In a journey full of many memorable incidents, the following adventures stand out: Brendan and crew visit St. Enda on the Aran Islands, then proceed west, where they come upon an island "full of hideous furry mice as large as cats." Next they come to two more amazing animal islands, one full of large, brilliantly white sheep and the other full of many "marvelous" birds. Then, dangerous water lulls Brendan's men to sleep; and just when all are growing despondent, "a bird alighted that moment on the prow of the ship, and made music sweet as an organ with its wings, beating them on the sides of the boat."

When Easter comes and it's time to find land and celebrate the Lord's resurrection, the men alight on an island that turns out to be a huge, hospitable whale. After Easter, the men resume their journey and the whale swims away, but the giant creature returns on schedule the next three Easters, allowing Brendan and his crew to celebrate the Eucharist on his body. Finally, after dodging a few dangerous whirlpools, Brendan and company return to Ireland.

And that was only the first lengthy journey! The second outing included encounters with demon dwarfs, nasty metalsmiths who tried to hurl molten metal at their boat, a fight between two sea monsters, a narrow escape from a menacing sea-cat, and a visit to a small island where Judas Iscariot, the betrayer of Christ, lived out his eternal torment. They also visited a mysterious island, the description of which in this translation of the *Voyage* by John J. O'Meara rivals Homer for sheer literary audacity:

One day when they had celebrated their Masses, a pillar in the sea appeared to them. . . . It was higher than the sky. Moreover, a wide-meshed net was wrapped around it. The mesh was so wide that the boat could pass through its openings. They could not decide of what substance the net was made. It had the color of silver, but they thought that it seemed harder than marble. The pillar was of bright crystal.

Some of the men cautioned against going too close to the mysterious island, but Brendan ventured forth, filled with a childlike curiosity about the world and a saint's faith in his sovereign God, telling his monks: "Let the boat in through one of the meshes, so that we can have a close look at the wonders of our creator." They then left the island and continued their journey.

Throughout their journeys, Brendan and his men risked drowning, faced being attacked by various sea monsters, and went for weeks without food or water, but they never gave up hope. Instead, they relied on a deep reservoir of faith in God. So strong was that faith that, at times, they sailed without using oars, sails, or tiller, relying solely on God to guide them. "Is not God the pilot and sailor of our boat?" Brendan explained. "Leave it to him. He himself guides our journey as he wills."

Finally, after nearly seven years of sailing, numerous hair-raising experiences, and visits to many beautiful islands full of remarkable birds and praying monks, Brendan and his men got to see the Land of Promise, which was everything they had hoped it would be. After landing, they were welcomed by a youth who greeted each of them by name and explained their delay in reaching the island: "You could not find it immediately because God wanted to show you his varied secrets in the great ocean."

Brendan's epic tale of seafaring and faith may have been written down within a few centuries of his death, and almost immediately it became a medieval best-seller, being read widely by saints and sailors throughout Europe. For centuries, people who believed Brendan actually did all the things recorded in his legend had little but faith to buoy them. Then, supporting evidence began to accumulate. When the Norwegians "discovered" Iceland in the 800s, they found Irish books and bells. Celtic monks had already landed there! Before Christopher Columbus sailed to America, he sailed to the Irish city of Galway in 1477, where he studied Brendan's journals and maps and recruited a Galway seaman for his planned Atlantic crossing. Until the 1970s, many scholars still loudly proclaimed that it would have been impossible for Brendan and his men to sail to America in one of the Irish monks' tiny leather boats, or coracles. They quieted down in 1977, when Tim Severin crossed the Atlantic using the same kind of boat that Brendan would have used.

Scholars will probably never stop debating where the fact in Brendan's legends ends and where the fantasy begins. Still, there's no doubting that Brendan is a potent symbol of the wanderlust that lies deep in the heart of Celtic Christianity. Brendan was far from the only Irish monk to sail the high seas following God's will.

❧ The love of travel

Where did the Celts—a people who had perhaps the strongest attachment to kin, clan, and their native land the world has ever seen—develop the taste for voyaging to the most remote parts of the world?

Perhaps their wanderlust was inspired by the life of

Jesus, for as Matthew tells us, "the Son of Man had nowhere to lay his head." There's additional biblical inspiration in the story of Abraham, the Jewish patriarch who was commanded by God to "Leave your country, your people and your father's household and go to the land I will show you." Or perhaps part of their wanderlust can be traced to St. Patrick, Ireland's roving patron saint, who was abducted from England and taken to Ireland, and then later voluntarily returned to wander throughout the country, preaching to the Celts in the island's remote, faraway places. We may look, too, to what Edward Sellner calls "their innate yearning to explore the unknown."

Although every major faith is full of pilgrimages and journeys, Christians in Celtic lands had a surplus of this urge to journey. Part of this yearning is probably not entirely different from the feeling modern tourists have for seeing previously unseen sights and cities. The Celts had this desire, too, and it was combined with a powerful love of the natural world, as well as a desire to visit Christian holy sites, both in the British Isles and in Europe. For the Irish, described by one of their saints as "denizens of the world's edge," traveling came with the territory. Their isolation on an island at the extreme western boundary of Europe required that they become excellent seafarers.

Christian Celts like Brendan and those who followed in his wake were also sent seaward by an urgent search for something they called "the place of one's resurrection." A uniquely Celtic concept that combines a Christian theology of the afterlife with the Celts' legendary love for the land, this belief held that God called everyone to a specific geographic location where he or she could experience a deeper sense of spiritual presence. And finally, there was also an evangelistic impulse. The Christian Celts sensed that they had a unique and powerful understanding of the Christian faith, and they felt compelled to take it on the road (or the seas), founding monasteries, communities, and churches wherever they went.

This divine restlessness often had a deeply ascetic character, and the Celts had a special term for it: White Martyrdom. This was a spiritual call to leave the known and familiar to head out into the unknown and often untamed lands. Lisa Bitel, author of *Isle of the Saints*, writes that the "Irish monks deliberately left their homes, kinfolk, and allies to seek sanctity in foreign wastes. They devoutly believed that their deaths in the wasteland . . . would bring spiritual rewards beyond anything they could find at home." Another writer states that in their self-imposed exile, the Celtic mystics were "crucifying their body on the blue waves." Or as Columban, one of the most widely traveled monks, put it, "Therefore let this principle abide with us, that on the road we so live as travelers, as pilgrims, as guests of the world."

🌀 Missions to far-off lands

If you look at a map of Europe, you can plainly see the lasting legacy of these Celtic pilgrims, who, from their small island outpost, sent hundreds of monks to re-Christianize the world. As they traveled throughout

France, Germany, Italy, and elsewhere, they founded monasteries along the way in an effort Celtic scholar Gerhard Herm calls "one of the great missionary feats of the church's history."

The most celebrated of all the Irish pilgrims to travel in Europe was Columban, who is also known by his Latinized name Columbanus, but is not to be confused with Iona's Columba. Columban's larger-than-life legend befits a saint who left his imprint on so much of the civilized world: He was reportedly rescued from drowning, freed from prison, and given power over wild wolves and bears, and there can be no doubt about his lasting impact. Irish author Sean McMahon writes in his book *Rekindling the Faith*, "he remains the great Irishman of Europe who relit the light that was not to be quenched."

Columban was a paradoxical figure who lived from around 543 to his death in 615. A poet who wrote many beautiful works, he was also an extreme ascetic who incorporated harsh punishments for minor infractions in the two monastic rules he wrote for communities he founded in Europe. Leaving Ireland in 591, Columban and his band of twelve Celtic monks landed first in France, where they established numerous monastic outposts. Most famous was Luxeil, located about two hundred thirty miles southeast of Paris at the modern-day city of Luxeil-les-Bains, which served as a hub for continental evangelism, becoming one of the great mother houses of European monasticism.

Soon, Irish monasteries were popping up like sunflowers across the French countryside. There were Angoulême on the Charente River in western France,

Péronne on the Somme River in northern France, Laon, which was seventy-five miles northeast of Paris, and Cologne, home of the famous monastery of St. Martin the Great. The monks also spilled over into what is now French-speaking Belgium, founding an important cathedral school at Liege.

They went to Germany, establishing centers at Aachen in the Westphalia region and Würzburg in Bavaria—a site that remains a popular destination for Irish pilgrims. They went to Austria, founding a monastery at an old pagan temple site at Bregenz, a town near Lake Constance near the border between Germany and Switzerland. They went to Switzerland, too, where a monk named Pirmin set up a center at Reichenau, located on an island in Lake Constance. St. Gall, one of Columban's original twelve disciples, elected not to cross the Alps with his hard-charging leader, and instead stayed put and created the important center of St. Gallen (or Sankt Gallen), located forty-five miles east of Zurich.

They went to Italy, founding Bobbio, a monastery fifty miles south of Milan, which was still going strong when St. Francis visited it in the early 1200s and is still open today. The Irish monks also established a center at Lucca, in Tuscany. And they also set up centers at Auxerre, Fiesole, Fulda, Lumieges, Regensburg, Rheinau, Trier, Salzburg, and Vienna.

▣ The wanderers

Columban and his band of pilgrim evangelists traveled to spread the Christian message, much as Patrick had done. Meanwhile, other Celtic monks were following the example of Brendan, who sometimes pulled up his oars and took in his sail to let God guide his ship to destinations unknown. In "The Voyage of Maeldune," a saintly legend with many similarities to Brendan's *Navigatio*, Maeldune tells his lost and lonely men, "Leave the boat quiet without rowing, and wherever God has a mind to bring it, let it go." These hardy holy men set out without any destination in mind, letting the winds and the will of God guide them, perhaps taking their clue from the mystical Gospel of John, which states, "The wind blows wherever it pleases. You hear its sound, but you cannot tell where it comes from or where it is going. So it is with everyone born of the Spirit." According to Anglican priest Michael Mitton, the Celtic Christians' willingness to wander was a part of their "total openness to the wind of the Spirit."

Even if we don't have all of the historical details, it's clear that such exploits were more than mere fantasy. The Anglo-Saxon Chronicle, one of a number of early British histories, reports that in 891 three Celtic monks "came to King Alfred in a boat without oars from Ireland whence they stole away, because they would be in a state of pilgrimage for the love of God, they recked not where." It's tempting to call monks such as these "aimless," but their aim was clear: to make themselves available to go wherever God would send them.

⊠ The pain of exile

It's hard for members of a mobile society like ours to understand how difficult it was for Celts to sever their ties to their loved ones and native lands and to set out for parts unknown. Whether they were the hard-charging evangelists like Columban, or the wandering mystics like Brendan, these pilgrim monks were defying millennia of cultural traditions and instincts by setting off from their homeland to serve God. In their own culture, criminals were punished with exile, which signals its terrors. And the Brehon laws, which had guided Irish society for centuries, declared that a person guilty of homicide should be cast adrift on the open sea if he could not pay the victim's survivors the compensation they deserved. Even a pillar of Celtic spirituality such as Columba, who left Ireland to found the monastery of Iona, seems to have never really gotten over his homesickness for his beloved native land. Although he pledged to stay away forever, he made at least one return trip to visit his monks at the monastery of Durrow.

The anxiety that all wandering monks must have sometimes felt was captured in the following prayer, which is attributed to Brendan:

Shall I abandon, O King of Mysteries, the soft comforts of home?

Shall I turn my back on my native land, and my face towards the sea?

Shall I put myself wholly at the mercy of God, without silver, without a horse, without fame and honor?

Shall I throw myself wholly on the King of Kings, without sword and shield, without food and drink, without a bed to lie on?

Shall I say farewell to my beautiful land, placing myself under Christ's yoke?

Shall I pour out my heart to him confessing my manifold sins and begging forgiveness, tears streaming down my cheeks?

Shall I leave the prints of my knees on the sandy beach, a record of my final prayer in my native land?

Shall I then suffer every kind of wound that the sea can inflict?

Shall I take my tiny coracle across the wide, sparkling ocean?

O King of the Glorious Heaven, shall I go of my own choice upon the sea?

O Christ, will you help me on the wild waves?

Today, one frequently hears the spiritual life referred to as a journey. Sermons and homilies are peppered with metaphors about life's long and winding road. What the Celts did was to turn this near-universal metaphor into a living reality. Lisa Bitel writes in *Isle of the Saints*, "The most profound expression of monastic spirituality, was to sever all social ties and march out of the gates of the sacred enclosure into the wilderness, never looking back. Irishmen became famous for the self-imposed exiles and pilgrimages that took them far from the security of home. The greatest heroes of Irish monasticism were vagrants."

This merging of metaphor with reality produced an

exhilarating faith that gave Celtic Christianity an urgency and expressiveness found in their prayers, prose, and poems. One can almost feel the rolling of the ocean and taste the salt water in the following tenth-century work by Cormac Mac Ciolionain, an influential king, bishop, and scholar:

> Wilt thou steer my frail black bark
> O'er the dark broad ocean's foam?
> Wilt thou come, Lord, to my boat,
> Where afloat, my will would roam?
>
> Thine the mighty: thine the small:
> Thine to mark men fall, like rain;
> God, wilt Thou grant aid to me,
> Who come o'er th'upheaving main?

⬚ From voyage to pilgrimage

In the County Mayo town of Westport in western Ireland stands a cone-shaped peak more than twenty-seven hundred feet high and visible for miles. Croagh Patrick is Ireland's holiest mountain. Tradition holds that Patrick spent forty days and forty nights fasting and praying on its rocky summit, beseeching God to give the Irish a special blessing. Historians say people have been climbing the mountain for thousands of years. Before the peak was consecrated by Patrick in the 500s, Celts honored the pagan god Lugh there. Ever since, making the climb has been believed to contribute to one's salvation. Today hikers and climbers use a path to ascend the mountain, but the footing is uneven and unstable. The mountain is covered with loose, jagged rock that gives way as soon as you put any weight on it.

That doesn't stop the approximately thirty thousand men, women, and children who climb Croagh Patrick every July as an act of religious devotion and spiritual pilgrimage. Many of the climbers ascend the rocky mountain barefoot, leaving their feet bruised and bloody. Even those who keep their shoes on have plenty of opportunities to get hurt: either from large hailstones, falling rocks dislodged by other climbers, or gale-force winds that make it seem as if you might be lifted off the face of the peak and dumped into beautiful Clew Bay below.

But climbing Croagh Patrick seems like a mere stroll when compared to the privations voluntarily undergone at Lough Derg in the northern reaches of County Donegal, a place of penitential pilgrimage that has been in use for at least a thousand years. The English government has made numerous attempts to prevent people from going there, but to no avail. So famous is this little lake, and the spiritual practices that go on there, that at the time when Columbus sailed to America in 1492, most world maps featured only Lough Derg in the whole of Ireland. The focus of attention there is an island called St. Patrick's Purgatory, where the saint supposedly had a vision of the afterlife. Today, more than thirty thousand people ferry out to the island, hundreds at a time, for a three-day vigil that includes fasting, sleep deprivation, and continual rounds of prayer and meditation.

▧ pilgrim's progress

Pilgrimages, such as climbing Croagh Patrick or fasting and praying at Lough Derg, are the average person's alternative to Brendan's seven-year voyage, and they show that anyone can take a journey for God. Some critics, however, think these journeys are unfortunate throwbacks to a medieval mindset. Irish journalist Liam Fay writes disparagingly: "If the Croagh Patrick climb were anything other than a religious ritual, there would be calls for it to be banned." There were complaints in Brendan's day, too. "It's better to stay piously put in one place than to wander around," wrote one saint. Others claimed the desire to wander came from the Devil and demons of wanderlust. In time, measures were put in place to limit monks' travels, and those who wandered without the consent of their abbots were disciplined.

Still, Celtic Christianity will always be remembered as a faith on the move, not a creed for couch potatoes. As they traveled for God, the Celts articulated an elaborate theology of the spiritual journey that continues to bless and inspire travelers to this day. There was St. Brigid, who was honored as the patron saint of pilgrims and travelers. There were miracles that protected pilgrims on the seas as well as roads, such as the time St. Aidan poured oil on rough waters, calming the waves and sparing the lives of some seasick monks. There were numerous prayers for protection on a journey from daunting obstacles like aggressive attackers and devouring animals. And there were hymns, like this one, which was reportedly sung by Columba during one of his travels: "There is no one could put an end to me though he should chance upon me in danger; there is no one could protect me the day my life will come to its end. My life, I leave it to the will of God."

▧ Setting out on the journey

Such serene faith in the face of constant dangers and the threat of sudden death can give us all courage, no matter what journey lies before us in life or beyond. The Celtic saints were willing to go around the world if God wanted them to. Where are you willing to go for God? Here are some ways to test your road-readiness.

- **Seek God's guidance.** You'll never know where God wants you to go if you don't ask. It could be across the globe. It could be across the street. Or it could be that the only direction you need to go is closer to God. Begin making it your custom to ask for divine guidance before you begin your day or plan your week. Ask God to show you what's most important.

- **Go somewhere for God.** You go to the grocery store for food. You go to the convenience store for gas. Where do you go for God? Consider giving somebody a ride, even if it's not on your way. Think about taking food or other necessities to someone who is doing without. Make yourself available to travel to do God's will.

- **Take your own pilgrimage.** Celts took both long journeys and shorter pilgrimages. In both cases, the physical travel was a means of achieving a spiritual aim. Consider making a pilgrimage of your own. This could be a trip to a recognized sacred site, or it could be a drive to a cabin where you can be alone with yourself and with God to take inventory of your life. Regardless of where you go, make plans to go somewhere for God.

11

THE LOVE OF LEARNING

Better far than praise of men
'Tis to sit with book and pen.

—poem by ninth-century Irish monk

The Book of Kells, a dazzling collection of texts from the New Testament Gospels and mesmerizing painted decoration, is one of the Western world's most prized ancient masterpieces. It's also a powerful symbol of the blossoming of art and literature that accompanied the rise of Celtic Christianity in Ireland and other lands.

Many of the major Celtic monasteries housed scriptoria, rooms or huts where monks performed the painstaking work of copying and illustrating manuscripts. Although they copied both sacred and secular works, they lavished their most luxurious illustrations on biblical collections, which moved one awe-struck twelfth-century observer to write:

Here you can look upon the face of the divine majesty drawn in a miraculous way . . . if you take the trouble to look very closely, and penetrate with your eyes to the secrets of the artistry, you will notice such intricacies, so delicate and subtle, so close together, and well-knitted, so involved and bound together, and so fresh still in their colorings that you will not hesitate to declare that all these things must have been the result of the work, not of men, but of angels.

The spectacular Book of Kells features dizzying images, which were designed to present basic Bible lessons to people for whom literacy was new. More an artifact of veneration than a document for reading, the book was at once a work of utter devotion to God and a testimony to the near-magical properties of the written word. In fact, dozens of the book's intricate illustrations feature books.

Almost every fact about the history of the Book of Kells is the subject of intense argument, but on some points there is the greatest agreement. Work on the book was begun sometime before 800 at Iona, the island monastery off the western coast of Scotland founded by Columba. But Viking raids forced the monks to hurriedly move the work-in-progress to the Kells monastery, some thirty miles northeast of present-day Dublin in County Meath. Monks at Kells continued working on the project during the ninth and possibly tenth centuries, but for some reason they never completed it, as some of the book's blank pages and unfinished illustrations confirm. Then, the book seemed to disappear, only to reappear centuries later; miraculously about ninety percent of the book was preserved from the elements,

Viking invaders, and the ravages of time. Around 1653, the governor of the town of Kells feared that Cromwell's British army might do what the Vikings hadn't, and sent the book to Dublin for safekeeping. Within a few years, it made its way to Dublin's Trinity College, where it has been carefully guarded ever since.

Bernard Meehan, Keeper of the Manuscripts at Trinity, notes that the artwork in the Book of Kells "combines high seriousness and humor." Each of the four gospels begins with a full-page illustration of the four evangelists: Matthew, Mark, Luke, and John, and there are full-page illustrations of Christ as well as the Virgin and Child. Meehan estimates that each of these illustrations may have taken a month to execute. One of the most frequently recurring visual motifs in the Book of Kells is that of Christ as a blond-haired, wide-eyed youth who sometimes looks more like a suntanned surfer than a suffering savior. There are also numerous crosses, angels, and Eucharistic chalices.

But not every image that appears is biblically inspired. Most of the pages of the book consist of beautiful script surrounded and interwoven with playful illustrations of humans and animals, along with the same kind of entwining abstract geometric patterns and spirals that appear on Celtic crosses and metalwork. Many of the illustrations show human figures, some contorted into unbelievably fluid yoga-like positions so they can fit into tiny spaces between the text, and others are intertwining or pulling each others' legs or beards. There are also numerous rodents, which may indicate that mice were the solitary monks' most constant companions. In one illustration, mice are seen carrying communion wafers in their mouths, and in another, a cat is chasing a mouse carrying a host.

While some of the illustrations are purely ornamental, many are intended to help interpret, clarify, or amplify the biblical passages they accompany. One slightly bawdy illustration, which appears alongside the lengthy genealogy of Christ at the beginning of Luke's Gospel, shows a bearded warrior holding a spear in one hand and a shield in the other, and between his legs, one can see an erect penis. Meehan believes the illustration is an allusion to the cyclical powers of procreation and death. We're not sure what the artist was thinking, but his drawing reveals that the Christian Celts hadn't lost some of their ancestors' earthiness and celebration of life.

The Book of Kells reveals a number of characteristics of the Christian Celts. For one, they were accomplished artisans. For another, their conversion to Christianity led to a flourishing of art and creativity, not an otherworldly disregard for the secular arts.

Before Patrick, most Celts observed a prohibition on writing. Within a century or two after Patrick, Irish became Europe's third written language. The effort the Celts put into incredible literary works like the Book of Kells shows that these formerly illiterate peoples took to words in a big way, and reveals that they placed a very high value on ideas and learning.

🎴 A flourishing culture

When one thinks of monasteries, one conjures up images of silent prayer and renunciation of the world. While some of the Celtic monasteries were indeed harsh places with ascetic practices, many were fertile ground for art and literature, which flourished throughout the Celtic lands. In addition to the Book of Kells, stunning illustrated Gospels were produced at Durrow and Lindisfarne.

Celtic cultures had always honored the bard and the storyteller, and in ancient times, the excellent wordsmith was nearly as revered as the king. The Christian Celts embraced this cultural imperative, drawing at least some of their inspiration from the opening passages of John's Gospel, which declared that Christ was the divine Logos: "In the beginning was the Word, and the Word was with God, and the Word was God." As Oliver Davies and Fiona Bowie write in their anthology, *Celtic Christian Spirituality*, "We find in Celtic Christianity a valuing of the creative imagination of the individual." For these new converts, "the creative arts stood not at the margins of the Church but at its very centre."

Monasteries became the incubators of this passion for learning. The most educated people of their time, monks taught the Bible, theology, and secular literature to anyone who was interested. Ciaran's Clonmacnoise, for example, was renowned as a great literary center, complete with a school, a scriptorium, and a library of religious and secular texts. The monks of the monastery even created a wonderful nonreligious fable called the "Book of the Dun Cow," as well as many annals, or early histories, of the region.

The growth of monastic schools, combined with the monks' proclivity for wandering, meant that many monks traveled from center to center, studying with other monks and taking advantage of the monasteries' open-handed hospitality. For centuries, monks taught young boys how to read, how to paint, how to play musical instruments, and how to memorize large chunks of the Bible. Even though hand-copied books were becoming more available, the monks still emphasized memorization, which had been a Celtic tradition for millennia. Over a period of years, students would be expected to memorize all one hundred and fifty biblical Psalms, as well as other religious and secular material.

The formerly bookless Celts began to avidly study just about anything they could read. This beloved poem, written by an anonymous ninth-century scribe, may help us understand their excitement:

> I and Pangur Ban my cat,
> 'Tis a like task we are at:
> Hunting mice is his delight,
> Hunting words I sit all night.
>
> Better far than praise of men
> 'Tis to sit with book and pen;
> Pangur bears me no ill will,
> He too plies his simple skill.
>
> 'Tis a merry thing to see
> At our tasks how glad are we,
> When at home we sit and find
> Entertainment to our mind.

Oftentimes a mouse will stray
In the hero Pangur's way;
Oftentimes my keen thought set
Takes a meaning in its net.

'Gainst the wall he sets his eye
Full and fierce and sharp and sly;
'Gainst the wall of knowledge I
All my little wisdom try.

When a mouse darts from its den
O how glad is Pangur then!
O what gladness do I prove
When I solve the doubts I love!

So in peace our tasks we ply,
Pangur Ban, my cat and I;
In our arts we find our bliss,
I have mine and he has his.

Practice very day has made
Pangur perfect in his trade;
I get wisdom day and night
turning darkness into light.

▨ Scribes and scriptoria

The nerve center of this Celtic intellectual ferment
was the scriptorium, and much of what we know about
this period comes from the pens of the scribes who

toiled there, and who wrote poems and notes in the margins of the works they were copying. The British novelist Stephen Lawhead, whose sprawling 1996 novel *Byzantium* begins at the monastery of Cenannus na Rig, which is Irish for Kells, vividly recreates this setting. In one scene of the book, the novel's central character, the monk Aidan Mac Cainnech, enters the monastery's scriptorium and examines a manuscript that has been the focus of his labors for days:

> Laying aside my pen, I sat in the empty room, looking and listening, remembering all that I had learned and practiced in this place. I gazed at the clustered tables, each with its bench, and both worn smooth, the hard, hard oak polished through years of constant use. In this room, everything was well-ordered and precise: vellum leaves lay flat and square, pens were placed at the top right-hand corner of each table, and inkhorns stood upright in the dirt floor beside each bench. . . .
>
> I saw the scriptorium [as] not a room at all, but a fortress entire and sufficient unto itself, a rock against the winds of chaos howling beyond the monastery walls. Order and harmony reigned here.

Lawhead's prose obscures the fact that life inside the scriptorium could occasionally be challenging, and often it was bone-chillingly cold. Work regularly shut down because the scribes' hands were too frigid to hold their pens still. Even in warm weather, the work was wearisome. One Irish monk wrote the simple complaint in the margin of a document he was laboriously copying: "This page is difficult. The third hour. Time for dinner."

Even though working with words could be hard, nothing could diminish the Celtic monks' passionate love affair with literature. They took their books and their love of learning with them wherever they went, and one of those who landed at the monastery of St. Gall in Switzerland wrote these simple lines, which describe how the consolation of literature was almost as pleasing as the comfort of the natural world:

> Over me green branches hang
> A blackbird leads the loud song;
> Above my pen-lined booklet I hear a fluting bird-throng.
>
> The cuckoo pipes a clear call
> Its dun cloak hid in deep dell:
> Praise to God for this goodness
> That in woodland I write well.

This flourishing of art and literature also shows that for much of the seventh, eighth, and ninth centuries, the Celtic monasteries enjoyed periods of relative peace and prosperity. Preparing the vellum and ink were major undertakings that required time, skill, patience and—in the case of some of the more exotic colors of ink that were used—trade with far-off lands. Vellum, which is treated calfskin, required hours of tedious work for monks who removed hair and debris with knives and solutions. Bernard Meehan estimates that the Book of Kells alone required the skins from some one hundred and eighty-five calves, which would have been culled from a herd of more than twelve hundred animals.

🪢 Bookish monks

In addition to copying sacred texts, the Celtic monks wrote original material, the bulk of it being the miracle-filled biographies of saints. Lisa Bitel says that over the course of six centuries, scribes composed hagiographies of hundreds of saints. These works were much different from contemporary biographies. In fact, in many of these fantastical works, there's no mention of some of the most basic facts of the saints' lives, such as the dates of their births and deaths, what they looked like, and the history of the communities they founded and directed. These biographies weren't meant to answer such questions. Instead, they were designed to instill faith, serve up saints as models of holy living, and win prestige for one monastery over another. Perhaps not surprisingly, the saints in many of these biographies loved literature.

The legends of St. Cuthbert, for example, describe his zeal for knowledge and learning. One time, after Cuthbert had been stricken with one of the plagues that periodically ravaged the countryside, he emerged from his illness healthy, but even more dedicated to learning all he could. When his mentor Boisil prophesied that his own death would occur in seven days, Cuthbert responded by saying, "Then tell me what is the best book to study; one that can be got through in a week." Boisil suggested the two study St. John's Gospel and commentaries on the book during their remaining days together.

After they completed their reading on the seventh day, Boisil "entered into the joy of eternal bliss."

The legends of Ciaran, founder of the important monastic school of Clonmacnoise, contained more than their share of bookish miracles. At one point, we are told, a fox carried Ciaran's Psalter for him. But in perhaps the most amazing literary miracle in the life of Ciaran or any other Celtic saint, a clumsy monk dropped Ciaran's Gospels into a lake, where they remained submerged for "a long while." Then, one day some cows went into the lake, and one emerged with the Gospels stuck to her hoof. Upon inspection, the book was dry as a bone, and not a single letter had been smudged.

St. Ninian, who evangelized the people of northern England and southern Scotland during the fourth and fifth centuries, liked nothing more than to relax with a good book. God granted him special bibliographic graces, so that his books remained totally dry, whether he was reading out in the British mist or even when studying during a driving rain. According to the "Life of Ninian," "When everything around him was soaked, he sat alone with his little book in the downpour, as if protected by the roof of a house." Only once did this protection fail. On a single occasion, Ninian's reading was interrupted when "an unlawful thought stirred in him and desire [was] prompted by the devil." Then and only then, a heavy rain deluged the reading monk and his book.

🔳 Columba and Columban: two towering literary figures

With its monastic schools and love of learning, Celtic Christianity produced more than its share of poet monks and scholar monks. Among the many, two figures stand out.

As we have seen, Columban spent his career wandering throughout Europe and founding nearly one hundred monasteries, work that led one writer to call him "the most intrepid of the intrepid Irish saints." In 1923, Pope Pius XI honored him for his efforts in re-Christianizing a desolate Europe, saying, "St. Columban is to be reckoned among those distinguished and exceptional men whom Divine Providence is wont to raise up in the most difficult periods of human history to restore causes almost lost."

In addition to his ceaseless traveling, Columban was an avid student of poetry, including his favorite writer, the Roman poet Ovid. Columban was also a prolific writer. Among his surviving works are biblical commentaries, two monastic rules, a number of letters, several sermons, and numerous poems, which he wrote in a learned Greek. One of these poems, "Carmen Navale" ("Boat Song"), was designed to be chanted by monks as they rowed their boats up the Rhine River.

As impressive as the career of Columban was, Columba—founder of the monastery at Iona where the Book of Kells was believed to have been created—is thought to be the foremost Celtic Christian scholar, writer, and poet. Columba was a prince who was born to an esteemed royal line. His great-great-grandfather was founder of the royal Ulster dynasty that continued uninterrupted into the seventeenth century. Raised in accordance with the customs for pagan royalty, he received his early schooling at the hands of bards and druids. And after his conversion, many referred to him as a "Christian druid." Columba spent nearly twenty years in ceaseless studying, preaching, teaching, and writing. "Columba never could spend the space of even one hour without study, or prayer, or writing, or some other holy occupation," wrote one of the saint's biographers. One legend says that he founded three hundred churches and wrote three hundred books, a claim that's impossible to document.

Adomnan's "Life of St. Columba" provides an intriguing portrait of this extraordinary saint and scholar. One of the most common images pictures Columba coming back to Iona from a round of preaching or a period of prayer, and returning to the solitude and study he loved. "When he had come down from the hill and returned to the monastery, he sat in his hut writing out a copy of the psalms," writes Adomnan in one of many such passages. To his biographer, Columba's knowledge and wisdom seemed so surpassing that any natural explanation for his learning was deemed unsatisfactory: "By divine grace he had several times experienced a miraculous enlarging of the grasp of the mind so that he seemed to look at the whole world caught in one ray of sunlight."

One episode from Adomnan's "Life" seems to especially support such a view of the power of Columba's intellect. It is a story that would warm the heart of any weary scribe:

One day Baithene came to St. Columba and said: "I need one of the brethren to help me go through the text of the Psalter I have copied and correct any mistakes." The saint said to him:

"Why do you bring this trouble on us when there is no need? For in your copy of the Psalter there is no mistake—neither one letter too many nor one too few—except that in one place the letter I is missing."

So it was. Having gone through the whole Psalter, it was found to be exactly as the saint predicted.

▨ "How the Irish saved civilization"

It's not often that books about ancient history spend more than a year on national best-seller charts, but then Thomas Cahill's delightfully engaging *How the Irish Saved Civilization: The Untold Story of Ireland's Heroic Role from the Fall of Rome to the Rise of Medieval Europe* is not your average book of history. "The word Irish is seldom coupled with the word civilization," writes Cahill in his opening chapter. By the time he concludes just over two hundred pages later, Cahill has proven his compelling argument that the Irish monks' appearance on the world's cultural stage at a crucial moment of human history allowed them to preserve much of what we now treasure as the high points of Western civilization. He states: "As the Roman Empire fell, as all through Europe matted, unwashed barbarians descended on the Roman cities, looting artifacts and burning books, the Irish, who were just learning to read and write, took up the great labor of copying all of western literature—everything they could lay their hands on [and] single-handedly refounded European civilization."

Cahill delights in the ironies that lie buried deep within this previously untold story, including the fact that the treasures of the world's culture would be saved by "outlandish oddities from a land so marginal that the Romans had not bothered to conquer it."

If it seems strange that the Irish were the saviors of civilization, some might find it even stranger that it was Christians devoted to the mission of evangelism who laboriously copied and saved books of Celtic pagan myths, anti-Christian Roman heresies, and skeptical Greek philosophers. Religious zealots aren't always known for their commitment to preserving other people's ideas, but the Irish monks copied it all. Occasionally, one of the Irish scribes would note his disagreements with a particular work in the margins as he worked, but as far as we can tell, these scribes faithfully reproduced their pages, regardless of their personal feelings.

The Celtic Christians combined a complex mix of devout religious faith and deep intellectual curiosity. Although monks like Columba and Columban disowned worldly wealth and creature comforts, they loved knowledge and cherished books. During their evangelistic journeys around the world, they would compare notes on philosophy and theology with one another and acquire books for their libraries back home, where scribes copied and distributed them. And as the wandering monks created monasteries and monastic schools all over the European continent, they took with them their love of learning and their skill in making and preserving books.

Irish monasteries may not have been luxurious, but they had well-stocked libraries. The Irish historian Peter Harbison notes: "Their libraries contained works descended from classical antiquity, not just the writings of Church Fathers, but of classical Latin authors as well, a number of which the Irish can claim to have preserved for posterity." Cardinal John Henry Newman referred to the Celtic monastic libraries as "the storehouse of the past and the birthplace of the future."

◼ A literary legacy

Our knowledge of the Celts' ancient past, as well as our understandings of the foundations of Western civilization, would be much poorer were it not for the curious monks. In addition to spreading the Christian faith throughout the world, these book-loving scholars also nurtured Celtic literary traditions, serving as a bridge between the ancient tales of the bards and druids and the blossoming of Irish literature that has occurred in the last few centuries.

In 1996, celebrated Irish poet Seamus Heaney won the Nobel Prize for literature, following fellow countrymen William Butler Yeats, who was awarded the prize in 1923, and playwright Samuel Beckett, who won in 1969. Heaney's poetry can be earthy and spiritual, and is often both at once. One of his earliest and best-loved poems, "Digging," opens with the young Heaney hearing his father sinking a spade into the ground beneath his bedroom window, and ends with the poet taking pen in hand and digging with it across clean, white pages.

These modern Irish writers stand on the shoulders of generations of earlier literary icons. James Joyce turned Dublin into a laboratory for his literary extravaganzas. In addition to *Dubliners*, his acclaimed collection of short stories, Joyce will be remembered for his moving *Portrait of the Artist as a Young Man*, which viewed the tensions of Catholicism and nationalism through a highly literary sensibility. He pioneered a modernist style that few have matched, both in his masterpiece, *Ulysses*, an epic novel that takes place in a single day in the life of Dubliner Leopold Bloom, and in his sprawling *Finnegan's Wake*. Along the way Joyce, who died in 1941, expanded the English language as well as the world's literary imagination, giving us such techniques as the now omnipresent "stream of consciousness" style.

John Millington Synge, whose *Riders to the Sea* may be one of the best-known works of Irish literature, remains a towering figure of twentieth-century drama; the Dubliner Oscar Wilde couched his stinging social commentary in gripping novels like *The Picture of Dorian Gray* and popular plays like *The Importance of Being Earnest*; Brendan Behan, a hard-drinking and tempestuous writer, turned out brilliant stories and plays before his death in 1964, and novelists Maeve Binchy and Edna O'Brien expose contemporary readers to the Irish experience.

The 1996 Pulitzer Prize for literature was also awarded to an Irish writer, Limerick-born memoirist Frank McCourt, author of the best-selling *Angela's Ashes*, a sad, touching, and humorous account of growing up in the midst of Ireland's grinding poverty. As he writes near the beginning of the book: "It was, of course, a miserable childhood. . . . Worse than the ordinary miserable childhood is the miserable Irish childhood, and worse yet is the miserable Irish Catholic childhood." According to Andrew Greeley, who may be America's best-loved Irish storyteller, Ireland has produced "more novelists, poets, storytellers, and playwrights per capita than any other country in the world."

▦ In search of wisdom

Celtic monks may have been bibliophiles, but they certainly weren't bibliomanes. Their love of books remained within healthy limits. For them, books were a means to the end of divine wisdom, and that wisdom was always seen as a different value from mere book learning. Monastic rules, such as "The Alphabet of Devotion," gave frequent warnings that "Wisdom which has no learning is preferable to learning without wisdom." In the same rule, a distinction is made between raw fact—which can be easily apprehended by anyone—and truth—which can only be grasped by the pure of heart:

> The right way to Truth.
> Should there be anyone who seeks truth, it is necessary for him that he really understand what hides it and what discloses it. Truth hides itself from those who despise it and shows itself to all who go all the way with it.

Truth is obscured by four things: illicit love and fear, indulgence and compulsion. In so far as a person remains unjust, he cannot herald the truth as it really is.

If they were around today, the Celtic monks would certainly draw a line in the sand between wisdom and things that to us sometimes seem to resemble it, at least superficially, such as "data," of which millions of us have unknown billions of bytes, or "information," on which most of us are overloaded. They would point instead to the Bible, which they saw as the world's preeminent book and the supreme source of divine wisdom. An early Celtic homily declares that holy scripture is a gift of God "by which all ignorance is enlightened, and all worldly sorrow comforted, by which all spiritual light is kindled, by which all weakness is made strong." The brief writings of St. Patrick alone, a short "Confession" and "Letter to Coroticus," contain nearly three hundred and fifty quotes from almost fifty different books of the Bible.

Nonetheless, the Celtic saints had a balanced appreciation for truth, some of which they believed could be derived from personal intimacy with God, some from studying scripture, and some from human literature. In a story from the life of St. Samthann, one day the saint received a visiting teacher who told her he planned to give up study and devote himself totally to prayer. "What then can steady your mind and prevent it from wandering?" she responded. Another saint recommended that "listening to the songs of clear-speaking poets" be a part of every devout person's spiritual practices.

Beyond the need for both temporal and spiritual teaching, the Celts believed that creating literature was a powerful way to honor the creator God. The very act of writing poetry could be seen as a form of prayer, as Welsh poet Cynddelw wrote, "Greatest Lord, take to yourself/This tribute of praise and well-formed poetry."

✠ Keep the light of learning burning

Today, we can carry on the Celts' deep love of learning with two simple activities that are as pleasurable as they are educational:

- **Read.** Chances are you already do this, but do you cherish books and learning as dearly as the Celts? With some fifty-thousand books published in America every year, as well as daily newspapers and magazines, there is no shortage of words. Browse the shelves of your local library or bookstore to see what new titles may interest you. You may want to form a book club to share your reading with others, or keep a journal of the books you've read and your thoughts about them. Whatever you do, keep reading, and while you're at it, thank God for the gift of language.

- **Write.** Some of the most beautiful pieces of Celtic poetry and prose were never meant to be preserved for centuries. In fact, they were never intended for any audience other than God. Rather, these random jottings were scribbled in a margin or written in a journal by a monk who was overcome by the beauty of an

Irish day. Do you ever grab a pen and a piece of paper and begin writing from the heart? Recapturing this Celtic tradition can be a profound way to reconnect with this spiritual practice.

12

Soul Friendship

Two shorten the road.

—Irish proverb

If you break a leg, you can call a doctor. If your car breaks down in the middle of the road, you can call a mechanic. There are millions of businesses you can call if you want someone to deliver a pizza, fix your plumbing, or invest your money in the stock market. But whom do you call when you need spiritual help? Who can perform the necessary repairs when it's your life that's broken?

The Celts had the answer. When they needed spiritual help or consolation, they turned to someone who was as close as a brother or sister, as loving as a mother or father, and as probing as a good psychoanalyst. They turned to a soul friend, who was their mystical mentor, their spiritual support system, their trusted guide on the road of life.

The Celts didn't create the idea of the soul friend, a concept that had been around for centuries in Christian teaching as well as the traditions of other faiths. What the Celtic Christians did was to elevate the importance of the soul friend to new levels. In fact, a popular Celtic saying claims: "Anyone without a soul friend is like a body without a head." If you've ever felt alone on your spiritual journey, the Celts have an important message for you about spiritual friendship.

Anatomy of a soul friend

The term *soul friend* comes from the Irish term *anam cara*, and means "one who shares my cell." Quite literally, soul friends were often cell mates, who prayed together and worked alongside each other during the day and slept in the same simple hut at night. Usually, the abbot of a monastery would assign an older monk or nun to look after and guide a younger brother or sister, so that one's soul friend was more than a roommate, and more like a personal mentor or minister. Most of the well-known Celtic saints had soul friends who helped and guided them. In turn, these same saints served as soul friends and mentors to others. Through this informal but influential network, the Celtic Christians passed on the faith and disciplined one another. The soul friend provided comfort or correction, as the situation demanded.

It's a concept that's as old as Solomon, who wrote in the biblical book of Proverbs that "There is a friend who sticks closer than a brother," and who waxed eloquent about the subject in Ecclesiastes:

Two are better than one,
because they have a good return for their work:

If one falls down,
his friend can help him up.
But pity the man who falls
and has no one to help him up!
Also, if two lie down together,
they will keep warm.
But how can one keep warm alone?
Though one may be overpowered,
two can defend themselves.

But perhaps no one has ever emphasized soul friendship so vigorously as the Celts. Cultural anthropologists will say there are good reasons for this emphasis deep in the Celtic character. As descendants of the Indo-European peoples who had roots in Asia, the Celts may trace their traditions to strong roots in Eastern religions, which place a heavy emphasis on gurus and other personal spiritual guides. In addition, Celts were accustomed to seeing their chiefs and kings seek out the local druid for guidance and counsel. Also, the traditional Celtic love of kin and clan would have made soul friendship seem like a natural way to live out the new Christian faith in Celtic lands.

Probably an even bigger contributor to the huge role that soul friendship played in the growth and spread of Celtic Christianity was the legacy of the desert fathers, those Middle Eastern hermits, monks, and mystics who fled to the desert in the fourth and fifth centuries and turned it into a garden of prayer and contemplation. St. Antony, one of the leading desert fathers, argued that having a soul friend could keep one from one of the consequences of solitude: "I know of monks who fell after much toil and lapsed into madness, because they trusted in their own work." According to Kenneth Leech, the twentieth-century Anglican priest, Celtic disciples streamed into the desert, where they "would seek out the advice and guidance of these holy men." A soul friend was often a wise older monk who was not merely someone who taught a spiritual technique, but "was a father who helped to shape the inner life of his sons through his prayer, concern, and pastoral care."

The lives of many Celtic saints exhibited this same combination of concern and care, and their biographies are full of stories about their relationships with their soul friends. For example Ciaran, the founder of the great monastery at Clonmacnoise, had a network of soul friends stretching across Ireland and beyond, including Enda, his mentor from the Aran Islands, Finian, a tutor from Clonard, and his closest soul friend of all, Kevin of Glendalough. One can imagine the warm embraces these brothers would have exchanged when they got together, and the lengthy conversations that would ensue about their communities, their travels by land and sea, and their spiritual journeys with God in the Christian life.

The bonds of soul friendship were lifelong. Legend has it that Ciaran and Kevin were so close that Ciaran's spirit reentered his body three days after his death so that he could once again share conversation and fellowship with his beloved friend Kevin. Findbarr of Cork, though known for his love of solitude and his solitary retreats on the island of Gougane Barra, was also a strong believer in soul friends. His biography says that Findbarr experienced deep anxiety after the death of Bishop Mac-

Cuirb, his longtime soul friend, and wondered whom he could share his joys and pains with now.

Inheriting the concept of the soul friend from the desert fathers, the Celts passed on their enthusiasm for soul friendship to monks in other lands. In later centuries, the practice would be warmly embraced by St. Bernard of Clairvaux, the twelfth-century French monastic leader, who wrote to the parents of a child who was joining one of his communities. "I will be for him both a mother and a father, both a brother and a sister," he assured. "I will make the crooked path straight for him, and the rough places smooth. I will temper and arrange all the things that his soul may advance and his body not suffer."

Qualities of the spiritual guide

From its humble beginnings in the deserts of the Middle East to its widespread adoption by the Celtic monks, the informal process of men and women finding other believers to act as soul friends became a more formal method that, over time, created a whole new group of religious leaders known as spiritual directors.

The relationship between the spiritual director and his sometimes numerous charges remained personal and intimate; but gradually spiritual direction began to look less like soul friendship, with its one-on-one relationship between a monk or nun and a cell mate, and more like a mentoring relationship. Instead of a partner or an equal, the soul director was a teacher who was believed to be superior in wisdom and godliness. A monk was expected to submit himself to such guidance. "He should place himself under the direction of an eloquent and devout man," says "The Rule of Cormac Mac Ciolionain."

The praiseworthy spiritual director—and the lives of Celtic saints say there were many such examples—combined the sage's mystical insight, the psychoanalyst's acute understanding of human nature, the priest's pastoral concern, and the abbot's discipline, as well as a saint's measure of patience, kindness, and love. He or she was a person of uncommon character and unquestioned spiritual integrity. St. Cuthbert, for example, sought out St. Boisil at Melrose to be his spiritual director because the older monk had a reputation for extraordinary virtue. Likewise, Hild of Whitby was sought out by many students because of her deep devotion to God and her reputation for chastity and charity.

Old Celtic monastic rules are full of guidance for both spiritual directors and those who would learn from their examples. "The Rule of Carthage," a lengthy and detailed monastic regulation that spells out the duties of bishops, abbots, priests, monks, and spiritual directors, has been attributed to St. Carthage, a seventh-century monk whose community grew to nearly nine hundred members. His "The Duties of the Spiritual Director" includes the following advice:

If you are a spiritual director to a man, do not
    barter his soul;
be not as the blind leading the blind; do not leave
    him in neglect . . .
Pay their dues of fasting and prayer; if not, you will
    have to pay

for the sins of all . . . Instruct the unlearned that
they may bend to your will.
Do not allow them to fall into the path of sin by
your example . . .
Do not be miserly with others for the sake of
wealth; your soul
is of more value to you than riches . . .
Yours is the duty of chanting intercessions at each
canonical hour
when the bells are rung . . .

Some monks proved unwilling to submit to such
guidance, as "The Rule of the Celi De" admits: "The office of a spiritual father is a difficult one since, when he
prescribes a true remedy, more often than not it is ignored. On the other hand, if the spiritual father does not
give advice, the culpability is his alone. . . . To point out
to them where salvation lies is always better, even if they
ignore the confessor's advice." Elsewhere, the same rule
instructs spiritual directors to "punish, correct, and
check" their students.

Apparently, the tendency of monks to ignore the advice of their spiritual directors was fairly widespread. At
the monastery at Tallaght, located just a few miles southwest of present-day Dublin, the thoughts of its founder
Maelruain were recorded by the hermit Mael Dithruib.
According to "The Rule of Tallaght," Maelruain:

used to say that the office of spiritual director was
perilous because, should the director impose on a
penitent a penance commensurate with the gravity
of the sin, it was more likely to be breached than

observed. But if the director did not impose a penance, the debts of the sinner would fall on himself.

If a monk repeatedly refused to obey his director, he was dealt with harshly. This was not only in order to maintain discipline in the community, but also to acknowledge that there were important spiritual issues involved in the ministry of direction. As "The Rule of Ailbe" states: "Anyone who will not accept correction, and who will not confess his fault, is to be sent about his business by his spiritual father."

The practice of giving spiritual direction did have its challenges, but it also had its tremendous successes. Because of this approach, hundreds of young believers received the opportunity to study and live with some of the outstanding saints of the Celtic lands. This, in turn, gave these students the best training available for living and teaching the Christian life, and it helped spread the Christian faith throughout the British Isles, as well as through much of Europe.

In later centuries, church leaders would further develop and refine the ministry of soul direction. In the eleventh century, St. Anselm received acclaim as an excellent spiritual director who could "analyze characters of every age and sex with such an accuracy that when he came to speak you perceived that he had lifted a curtain and was showing each one his own heart." In the twelfth century, a Dominican priest wrote that the spiritual director should be "inclined to correct kindly and to bear the weight himself. He must be gentle and affectionate, merciful to the faults of others. He is to help [his charge] by calming his fears, consoling him, giving him back hope, and, if need be, by reproving him. Let him show compassion in his words and teach by his deeds." And St. Francis de Sales, who lived in the sixteenth and seventeenth centuries, wrote that a spiritual director "must be full of charity, knowledge, and of prudence; if one of these three qualities is wanting in him, there is danger."

Through the centuries, the ministry of spiritual direction maintained the heart and soul of Christian charity that was developed by the desert and Celtic monks centuries before. As the Celtic proverb states, "A friend's eye is a good mirror."

Confession and accountability

There's yet another way that the Celtic tradition of soul friendship and spiritual direction had an influence far beyond the Celtic lands of the British Isles, and that's in the practice—later the sacrament—of confession. Although the Celts practiced confessing their faults to a soul friend or spiritual mentor, the act didn't require a priest. But after the seventh century, as churches across Europe gradually adopted the Celtic practice, they increasingly made confession a matter between an individual and a clergyman. This practice was officially adopted as a sacrament by the Catholic Church at the Lateran Council in 1215.

Many of the early Celtic Christians probably wouldn't recognize the sacrament of confession as it has been practiced in recent centuries. Nor would they know what to make of confessional booths. They would, however, applaud the recognition of the need to confess sins and failures not only to God but to fellow brothers and sisters, as has been a part of Christian practice since the earliest days, when James the brother of Jesus urged his followers to "confess your sins to each other and pray for each other so that you may be healed."

Many of the major Celtic monastic rules urged monks to confess their sins to fellow monks or to their spiritual director. "The Rule of Ailbe" states, "After vigils, let each monk listen, while prayerfully and steadfastly confessing his sins." Elsewhere, the same rule claims the healing impact of the practice. "Let each confess his sins before the cross and in the presence of the abbot, with humility and without excusing himself, that so the demons may not have cause for rejoicing."

Here, as elsewhere in the monks' teaching, one encounters the idea that confession is a liberating experience that both washes one clean of past errors and helps prevent future failings. Designed neither to humiliate the confessor nor to give him a false sense of security, confession helped those who were sincerely trying to follow God more closely to realize the gravity of their sin and deny sin a foothold.

For those who believe that confession is the spiritual equivalent of a "Get out of jail free" pass, allowing someone to commit crimes knowing that there will be a liberating loophole down the road, numerous passages in the Celtic monastic rules make it clear that this was not the intention of confession. "The Rule of Tallaght" makes it clear that Maelruain believed "Frequent confessions, followed by equally frequent lapses into sin, he considered useless unless one carried out the prescribed penance." And "The Rule of the Celi De" warned: "Frequent confession is useless if the transgressions are also frequent."

In practice, the only thing that separates meaningful confession from empty ritual is the sincerity of the penitent. Today, when some overworked priests may hear dozens of confessions in a single day, ascertaining people's true motivations may be difficult. But in the Celtic monasteries, where one enjoyed a close relationship with a soul friend or spiritual director, confession served as a powerful tool for strengthening spiritual resolve and helping free people from the clutches of sin.

The Celts valued communalism as highly as we prize individualism. While to many of us, such submission might be viewed with suspicion, for them, submitting to a respected spiritual leader seemed completely natural. Celtic spiritual leaders operated like good parents. Though they attempted to direct their students' lives, they did so without breaking their wills. Their directives depended on the consent of their charges, not the unquestioned spiritual authority of the leader. As Thomas Cahill writes, "Personal conscience took precedence over public opinion or church authority."

The ultimate authority in all matters rested with God, not with a human figure. Or as St. Findbarr of Cork often said, the only and ultimate spiritual guide is the Holy Spirit. Through their practice of spiritual direction, the Celts tried to find a way to let the older, wiser brothers and sisters guide those who hadn't traveled as far on the spiritual journey. The goal of all such direction was to guide people to God, not encumber them in human rules and regulations.

🜏 No one is an island

The English poet John Donne has famously written "No man is an island entire of itself; every man is a piece of the continent, a part of the main." Although the journey to God is a deeply personal one, many lessons are learned best in concert with other pilgrims. The spiritual life isn't a solo performance; it's more like a symphony, in which the various instruments play an important role in creating the beauty and harmony of the whole. Here are some suggestions to guide you along the way.

- **Find a soul friend.** At one time or another, nearly everyone has felt the desire to have someone come alongside and give hope and guidance. Friends are helpful, and parents and priests are invaluable. But the soul friend is a unique person who can provide comfort when needed and correction when you're heading off course. The job doesn't require supernatural insight, just a willingness to listen and be vulnerable about the deep issues of life, and provide guidance to a fellow traveler when possible. Why not ask God to give you a soul friend? Then keep your eyes open to the gift in your life.

- **Be a soul friend to someone else.** You may not think of yourself as a spiritual giant, but you don't have to be a spiritual superstar to help someone else. All it takes is a compassion for someone who may be struggling and a willingness to listen and to share the lessons that have helped you grow and mature. If you feel you could help another, why not make yourself available?

- **Practice servant leadership.** No one likes a know-it-all, but people are attracted to someone who exhibits grace and the willingness to give. Ask God to let you be a helper to others, and you'll be surprised at the opportunities that will present themselves. Be willing to be a servant. Or as St. Paul said, "Be devoted to one another in brotherly love. Honor one another above yourselves."

13

CARE OF THE SOUL

Before setting forth on that inevitable journey, none is wiser than the man who considers—before his soul departs hence—what good or evil he has done, what judgment his soul will receive after its passing.

—Cuthbert, abbot of Jarrow

In 1699, Irish landowner Charles Campbell hired local workers to help him build a road. He asked the men to remove some stones from a nearby mound. After hefting a particularly large slab, the men found themselves looking into a deep, dark passageway. Although they didn't know it at the time, the workers had discovered Newgrange, an ancient monument more massive than England's Stonehenge and hundreds of years older than Egypt's pyramids.

Constructed of tons of hand-carried earth and hundreds of huge, heavy stones, Newgrange is one of the most sophisticated engineering projects ever completed. At a time when the life span of the average human was less than thirty years, construction of such megaliths (meaning "large stone") must have involved many generations of workers and required millions of man hours of highly organized labor. In addition, building materials would have been transported over lengthy distances. The brilliant white quartz that decorates the front of Newgrange was brought some forty-three miles from the Wicklow hills. The water-rolled granite stones that protrude from the quartz traveled more than thirty miles from the area around present-day Dundalk. And the nearly one hundred large, rectangular curbstones that once circled the mound were carried nearly ten miles—an incredible feat since some weigh many tons.

Beyond the astonishing mechanics of its construction, Newgrange has a mystique that inspires awe and wonder. It's long been believed to be the burial place of many of Ireland's High Kings of Tara and is the setting for much ancient Celtic mythology. For Newgrange is more than a pile of rock and dirt. It's also a timeless tomb, a massive memorial to the dead. It remains, as one writer called it "perhaps the most celebrated and enigmatic sacred monument on earth." As such, it's one of the earliest and most striking testimonies to the near universal human belief in an afterlife and the existence of the soul.

Built more than five thousand years ago by an ancient pre-Celtic people whose own simple houses and huts have long since vanished, Newgrange demonstrates that its builders placed a premium on honoring the dead. Archaeologists, who spend their time examining the physical remains of prehistoric people, know that they've discovered human activity when they uncover remnants of ancient art and architecture. But when they discover something like Newgrange, they know they've found evidence of a culture that held some kind of belief in an afterlife.

Belief in the existence of the soul and its survival after the body's physical death is one of the building blocks of just about every faith known to humanity. The people who labored to construct Newgrange had a belief in the immortality of the soul that was at least as solid as the heavy rocks they used to make this majestic monument, and they were not alone in their faith. More than twelve hundred megalithic tombs dot the Irish countryside, and Newgrange is just one of an estimated twenty thousand ancient burial monuments that exist throughout the regions of Europe once inhabited by the Celts.

⬛ Anatomy of an ancient tomb

Standing guard upon a ridge top, Newgrange overlooks the sacred River Boyne—believed to be the home of the goddess Boann—just six miles west of where the river flows into the Irish Sea. The monument is surrounded by a dozen large standing stones, the remnants of a thirty-five-stone circle that once enclosed a sacred space of nearly two acres. The immense tomb itself weighs hundreds of tons, stands nearly forty feet high, and spreads over an area that's three hundred feet in diameter. Such a project would be considered massive using modern earth-moving equipment, but one can hardly imagine how it was erected five millennia ago with little more than muscles and sweat. In fact, Newgrange is so huge and its engineering so sophisticated that archaeologists long thought it the product of a more recent age.

But the real triumph of Newgrange lies deep under the mass of earth and stone. A narrow, sixty-foot passageway takes the visitor through a corridor consisting of more than twenty pairs of huge stones that serve as the passage's walls. The hall leads to a cross-shaped tomb area, featuring a central chamber that can hold more than twenty visitors.

The ancient architects who designed Newgrange proved to be expert builders. To construct the roof, they used a primitive but efficient method called corbelling, which involved laying rock slabs on top of each other, with each new slab extending slightly over the lower slab until they met in the center, creating a roomy chamber nearly twenty feet tall. The ingeniously slanted stones are carved with tiny drainage channels that have successfully diverted rainwater from the chamber for five thousand years.

Radiating off the central chamber are three smaller burial niches. Newgrange was vulnerable to looters for centuries, so it's hard to tell what the tomb's original contents were. But when archaeologists began work on the monument in the 1960s, they found a large ceremonial stone basin and the cremated remains of three or four people. Newgrange was thus clearly a communal burial site, not a monument to a single king, like the pyramids of Egypt.

From its massive stone supports to its protective slab roof, Newgrange is a model of efficient and purposeful design. But the monument isn't merely functional. Many of the stones inside and outside the tomb are decorated with strikingly beautiful and surprisingly contemporary-looking abstract carvings, dozens of spirals and circles, numerous wavy lines, and many other geometric patterns. The most remarkable designs—and the subject of great debate—are the triple spirals decorating the giant stone that stands outside the entranceway to the tomb's inner chamber. Some see in these carvings universal symbols of eternity and the afterlife. Others believe they represent a map of Newgrange and some of the surrounding sacred sites.

Regardless of their precise meaning, the inclusion of so many artistic flourishes shows that the tomb's builders wanted to create a monument that was more than merely functional. Their flair for extravagant embellishment affirms that people are different from dirt, rocks, plants, and animals in a spiritually significant way.

The promise of new life

Tombs don't talk, and while we can be thankful that the once-Celtic countryside has so many thousands of ancient remains, we can also be frustrated at how little we know about the people who lived so long ago and about the reasons they created these mysterious sites. We know ancient people built monuments to honor the dead, but we'll probably never know much about the beliefs that inspired them or the rituals and celebrations that moved them. No written records have been found before those dating thousands of years after the construction of Newgrange, and everything earlier than the fifth century is pretty much relegated to the mysterious and impenetrable mists of prehistory.

But in the 1960s, archaeologist M. J. O'Kelly made a fresh discovery that shed new light on the Newgrange tombs. During reconstruction of the monument's fallen outer walls, O'Kelly had puzzled over the purpose of a small rectangular opening, called the roof box, that was positioned above the entranceway to the tomb's passage. Some researchers had speculated that the roof box was a ritual device, used by the living to pass food to the dead after the tomb had been sealed, but its true purpose had never been fully agreed upon.

Then early one winter morning while O'Kelly was working deep within the tomb, he was enlightened. As he toiled in the darkness, the gloom was pierced by a thin ray of light shining in through the roof box. After further research, O'Kelly concluded that Newgrange's architects had designed the monument to be a huge solar receptor, built with an orientation toward the rising sun on the winter solstice. During this shortest day of the year, which falls on December 21, the sun streams into Newgrange's central room for a full seventeen minutes, illuminating the chamber of death with a brilliant, life-affirming light.

It's hard for us to imagine what the ancient Celts made out of the movements of the stars across the expanse of the sky. Today, precise atomic clocks help us subdivide and domesticate time. And whether we're asleep in our beds, working at a computer, or driving in a car, we're never far away from a digital readout showing us the time in crisp-looking hours and minutes. But our ancestors measured time in more natural ways: by the movement of planets and the changing of the seasons.

Practical experience and the words of local wise men taught early humans to expect that the sun would rise again in the morning after it had set at night, just as they knew that the short, cold days of winter would again be followed by the long, warm days of summer. But throughout the ancient world, monuments like Newgrange helped people make sense of the vast machinations of the cosmos. These monuments of earth and stone affirmed that the universe was regulated and reliable.

Every December 21, when the golden rays of the morning sun traveled down Newgrange's narrow, sixty-foot corridor and illuminated the chamber area within, the beliefs of the surrounding community were affirmed. For just as the setting of the sun was part of the cycle of the days, and the cold of winter was part of the cycle of the seasons, so—they believed—death was just a stage in the cycle of life. If there was a message to Newgrange, it was that human life would continue on, in some form, just as the summer sun would again warm the fields.

▦ The people of the tombs

Standing in the inner chamber of Newgrange is a moving experience for the many thousands who venture deep into the bowels of the tomb. One has a pervasive sense of timelessness, as well as a sense of awe for the ancient architects who painstakingly constructed it. Looking up to the corbelled roof twenty feet above, one is amazed that the roof can hold its massive bulk and weight. (And one hopes that it will continue to hold for at least a few more minutes.) Then, when the tour guide turns off the lights, letting the visitors' eyes adjust to the darkness before turning on a small lamp that simulates the effect of the winter sun creeping into the chamber, one can see why people make reservations years in advance for the opportunity to stand in the chamber during the winter solstice.

While Newgrange is the pre-Celtic people's most impressive monument to the dead, it's far from the only tomb in town. A cluster of smaller satellite tombs can be found just outside. Another constellation of graves is nearby to the north, with a central tomb called Knowth surrounded by nearly a dozen smaller tombs, and a mile or two east of Newgrange lies a tomb called Dowth. Newgrange, Knowth, and Dowth make up the Boyne necropolis, a network of ancient tombs that share certain structural similarities and are visible one from another. All three of these tombs had fallen out of use by the time the Celts fanned out across Europe and the British Isles in the centuries before Christ, but the Celts built hundreds of their own tombs, in which they carefully laid the dead and surrounded them with goods they believed would be required in the afterlife. One famous Celtic tomb holds a warrior figure, buried in full military dress and sitting in a regal chariot. Other tombs house the dead along with numerous household items, which presumably would be needed in the afterlife.

The druids, the Celts' spiritual leaders, never committed their views to writing, but scholars credit them with being one of the first groups to develop a consistent body of teaching about the immortality of the soul.

From what we've been able to piece together, the druids taught that the underworld, a realm inhabited by the dead, had many parallels to normal life and could sometimes be visited by the living.

In addition, early Celtic artists hint at their views of the afterlife in their sculptures and metalwork. The famous Gundestrup Cauldron, a silver-plated bowl from the first century A.D. seen by many as a precursor to the fabled Holy Grail of Arthurian legend, is decorated with the images of various deities and mythical scenes. But one panel contains an image many say represents the cycle of death and rebirth. One row of Celtic soldiers appears to be marching from left to right on the surface of the earth, when they meet their death and fall to a lower level, where another row of soldiers seems to be marching right to left in the underworld until they are reborn again on the earth.

It's extremely risky to make sweeping theological deductions from tombs and buried treasures, even though many writers seem more than willing to take the risk. But one thing is clear: As the Celtic people migrated across Europe, they left thousands of memorials to their dead, showing conclusively that they didn't believe physical death was the end of the story.

■ The ultimate sacrifice

On August 1, 1984, a farmer cutting peat in the English countryside thirty miles east of Liverpool found a well-preserved human leg. An archaeologist who heard about the discovery rushed to the site, known as Lindow

Moss, where he discovered a small flap of skin sticking out of the peat. Soon, excavators set upon the site, where they found a man's torso. Radiocarbon dating techniques suggested the man had been buried in the bog for two thousand years. As scientists at the British Museum cleaned and studied the body, they made a series of surprising discoveries, which increasingly supported the idea that his death had been part of a Celtic ritual sacrifice.

First, the man's skull had been fractured with some kind of ax-like implement, perhaps rendering him unconscious. Next, his neck had been broken as if he had been hung, and a strand of animal sinew was wrapped so tightly around his neck that it had cut deeply into the flesh. Finally, his throat and jugular vein had been slit using a sharp blade wielded with almost surgical precision.

The use of sacrifices, both animal and human, to in some way make a connection with the divine, was a near-universal element of ancient religions. The Aztecs offered plants, animals, and humans in an effort to maintain the invisible order of the cosmos. Hindus engaged in sacrifice as a way to please or appease various goddesses. In China, sacrifices of the living as well as offerings of jade, silk, and a variety of culinary delights were made to various ancestral deities or to deities ruling over the seasons, lakes and mountains, or the stars. And sacrifice is a central motif of Judaism, from the propitiatory rituals involving sacrificial lambs to Abraham's attempted sacrifice of his son, Isaac.

Today, we may look back at all this blood-soaked carnage with disdain, wondering how the human pursuit of wisdom and truth could be the source of so much brutality and bloodletting. Certainly, that's how the Romans felt when they first stumbled upon the Celts' sacrificial rituals. But ironically, these Romans were conveniently ignoring their own rituals of bloodletting, where thousands of spectators crowded into the innocuously named Roman Circus, to watch gladiators duel to the death, defenseless victims be mauled by wild animals, and Christians and other social undesirables be fed to waiting lions.

Although rituals of human sacrifice are just about universal in ancient cultures, it's impossible for us to know what it was that the early Celts were trying to accomplish with sacrifices like that of the so-called Lindow Moss man and the uniquely Celtic practice of the "triple death." Bodies preserved in peat for two thousand years tantalize us with clues, but in the end they don't speak any more clearly than rocks or tombs.

We do know that the concept of sacrifice was an important part of the teaching of the first Christian missionaries to the Celtic people. Christianity, which replaced Judaism's system of repeated sacrifices with the once-and-for-all sacrifice of the promised Messiah, took seriously the Celtic insistence on the necessity of propitiation. But instead of requiring a steady stream of victims' blood, Christianity proclaimed that the blood spilled by Jesus was sufficient for all.

Ultimately, even though the builders of Newgrange and Ireland's early Christian teachers had significantly different answers to the questions of life and death, both groups affirmed that ultimately, life doesn't end. Although the Christian concept may have sounded alien to the Celtic ritual leaders, one can be sure that it was welcomed warmly by those who were scheduled to join the Lindow Moss man in the triple death.

❧ The art of dying

Much has changed since Newgrange was built five thousand years ago. Today, medical science has explained much more about the causes of death, and it can even help extend and sustain life, so that we now live an average of two to three times longer than the Celts did. Still, nothing has changed the inevitability of death, which then, as now, is one of the few certainties of life.

The ways in which people die have certainly changed over the millennia. Ancients didn't have to worry about plane crashes or electrocution. Today, few people are devoured by a wild boar (or attacked by a wild Celt). But regardless of which century they inhabit, humans usually believe that the death is an untimely anomaly, not a fact of life that could happen for any of us at any moment. Research will undoubtedly continue into antiaging medications and numerous potions designed to camouflage the wrinkles that accompany advancing years.

Still, so far no one has come up with a concoction to postpone death, and the wisdom of the ages teaches that it's probably better not to try. One tenth-century Irish poet warned, "Avoiding death/takes too much time, and too much care,/when at the very end of all,/Death catches each one unaware." The Celtic monks of the fifth, sixth, and seventh centuries lived lives of rigorous discipline that were a kind of daily death. Their scribes wrote often of death's inevitability, and a passage from

"The Rule of St. Comghall" of Bangor advises, "Let the monk daily bear in mind that he will die."

Of course, one needn't morbidly court death, for it will come in due time, and one shouldn't tempt death, for it may strike sooner than we like. But the Celtic people—whether pre-Christian souls, who lived amongst the tombs and remains of the dead, or Christian believers, who celebrated the resurrection of a crucified savior—agreed that one needed to factor the inevitability of death into the mathematics of daily life.

In contemporary Ireland, the living don't bury the dead in backyard mounds, but many commemorate the passing of loved ones from this world to the next with the lengthy and noisy tradition of the wake. Andrew Greeley, highlighting the origin of this practice in the pagan belief that guarding a body through the night would ward off evil spirits and aid its journey to the afterlife, writes that these rituals "are, to describe them precisely, celebrations of a faith (older than Christianity but strongly reinforced by Christianity) that life is stronger than death." The Irish today, who are the inheritors of centuries of honor for the dead, make funerals into grand gatherings of family and kin, where tales of the deeds of the dearly departed are recounted to waves of tears and toasts. The old Irish ballad "Tim Finnegan's Wake" recounts the boisterous goings-on that can still be found at Irish funerals:

> Whack for the da now,
> Dance to your partner
> welt to the floor
> your trotters shake

 wasn't it the truth I told you
 Lots of fun at Finnegan's wake.

 Or, as Frank McCourt writes in *Angela's Ashes* about growing up in Ireland, "There's nothing like a wake for having a good time."

🪷 The art of living

Few people would argue that the purpose of life is to be celebrated with a memorable funeral, or to be buried in a glorious tomb. Such niceties don't alter the eternal destiny of the dead so much as they open the eyes of the living. And if they're successful, they inspire us to live our present lives in a way that takes the next life seriously.

Unfortunately, too many people live a soul-denying existence. Although few are card-carrying philosophical materialists, many live as if matter is more substantial than spirit, time more meaningful than eternity, the here-and-now more meaningful than the immortal. The Celtic author of "The Rule of Ailbe" warned his monastic disciples that "The good of your soul should take precedence over the good of your body." Hinduism describes humans as lost in "maya," a veil of demonic deception that keeps us confused about spiritual truth. The ancient Celts expressed the same theme in a language they found more familiar, comparing shortsighted humans to animals caught in snares. A centuries-old [Celtic] prayer urges God to protect us from investing our lives in things of relatively little value: "That we may not barter the true light and true beauty of the life eternal for the deceitful fantasy of the present life."

Much in life is so uncertain. No one knows tomorrow's weather, next week's stock prices, or next year's political climate. But one thing is certain: You will surely die. For most people, death comes at a time not of their choosing. For way too many, death comes before they're prepared. The message that echoes from the somber stillness of Newgrange and a thousand other ancient tombs is that the present is our best—and perhaps our only—time to prepare.

preparation for the inevitable

There are numerous ways that we today can begin applying the wisdom of the Celts to the timeless interplay between life and death.

- **Experience death at close range.** Irish wakes, with all their jollity and revelry, are still events that at their core are somber recognitions of the reality of death. Unfortunately, much of the Western world deals with death in ways that are designed to mask its frightful finality. You may be given an opportunity to attend a traditional Irish wake. If not, go to a funeral with all your senses activated. Listen to the bereaved. Are their eyes full of sorrow at a life that failed to measure up? Or are their hearts full with an ethereal kind of joy that they are fortunate to have spent part of a lifetime with the dearly deceased? What does the priest or preacher say, and what is left unsaid? This sensitive kind of attention to the reality of death will help your own immortality sink in.

- **Picture death as a beginning, not an ending.** The

Venerable Bede, a beloved eighth-century monk at the British monastery of Jarrow who is often called the "Father of English History," recorded *A History of the English Church and People*, which is one of our best historical records of the Celtic church. When Bede sensed his own death approaching, he welcomed it with open arms as "a heavenly birthday." Bede's faith in things unseen overcame the fears that naturally resulted from seeing the only life he had known slowly ebbing away.

- **Take care of unfinished business.** Bede could welcome his death in part because of his clean conscience before his fellow men and women and his peace of mind before God. In what could be a testimonial for the practice of confession and the beauty of forgiveness, Bede kept short accounts with others and he stayed on his knees confessing his failures to God. As a result, when it came time to die, he had no huge backlog of unfinished business.

- **Get bigger.** Some people are profoundly offended by the idea that God would "send people to hell." But others look at hell not as a place where God sends people, but as a spiritual condition that is the natural inheritance of people who are selfish, shortsighted, and spiritually stunted. The key for these people is to get bigger, growing their souls to a larger fit-for-eternity size. As St. Colman wrote in his "Alphabet of Devotion," a classic Celtic Christian devotional work: "What is best for the soul? Humility and magnanimity. . . . What is most harmful to the soul? Narrowness, contention, and repression." Soul growth doesn't come easy. Some have learned from others more spiritually attuned than themselves. And some have learned key principles like love and compassion by venturing out of their comfort zone and serving the neglected and the needy.

- **Picture the future.** Throughout history, seers and visionaries claim to have been given direct access to the mysteries of the afterlife. Among this group, the Celtic saints Adomnan of Iona and Fursey, who was a missionary to England and France, wrote detailed accounts of their visions of heaven and hell that influenced Dante's *Divine Comedy*. Their visions also shaped medieval religious thought, and by extension, painters whose stunning portrayals of the afterlife graced chapels and cathedrals around the world, where they inflamed worshippers' imaginations with two contrasting visions of the soul's state after death. While both pie-in-the-sky and fire-and-brimstone can be abused, it helps to imagine where you want to wind up.

- **Look at life as a gift.** Imagine you gave a friend a pair of shoes that she wore for years before throwing them away in disrepair. Would you be sad when the shoes were retired after years of productive use? Likewise, some look at life as a gift that's given to us for our use for ten, twenty, or more years. Then, after our time on earth, we return to our source. That's the way things were seen by St. Columba, who was one of the best-known Celtic saints. About a week before his death in 597, his biographer reported seeing an angel visit the monks in chapel. "Look," said Columba, "an angel of the Lord, sent to recover a loan." Perhaps if we look at life as a gift rather than a possession or an entitlement, we'll be more gracious in the way that we live and the manner in which we die.

CELTIC SAINTS

Hundreds of holy men and women are honored by the Celtic people as "saints," even though few have been officially canonized by the Catholic Church. The ten listed below are among the most important.

BRENDAN (486?–575)

Founder of monasteries at Clonfert, which was one of Ireland's premier monastic schools and elsewhere, Brendan is best known for his amazing sea journeys recorded in fantastical detail in *The Voyage of St. Brendan*, a phenomenally popular medieval travelogue which was studied by Christopher Columbus. The best known among many wandering Celtic monks, Brendan reportedly had many death-defying adventures, including encounters with sea monsters, before returning to his home in beautiful County Kerry. Feast day: May 16. (See chapter 10.)

BRIGID (?–525?)

Also known as Brigit and Bride, this amazing woman is Ireland's most beloved saint, and is affectionately called "Mary of the Gaels." The founder of a famous double monastery for men and women at Kildare, little is known about this saint, whose numerous legends are interwoven with Celtic folklore, legend and myth. Her name is that of a pagan goddess of fire and song. Feast day: February 1, which is also the pagan holiday of Imbolc. (See sidebar pp. 94, 124.)

CIARAN (?–545?)

The founder of the famous monastic center at Clonmacnoise in central Ireland, Ciaran was a disciple of Enda of Aran and Finian of Clonard. Although he died a few months after establishing his monastery, its influence continued for centuries as a center for learning and art. Feast day: September 9. (See pp. 132–133, 198–200.)

COLMAN (?–670?)

When Catholic leaders tried to force Celtic Christians to submit to their authority, Colman, bishop of the monastery at Lindisfarne, refused. Formerly a monk at Columba's island monastery of Iona, Colman was known for his deep piety and intellect. He retreated to Inisboffin Island off the western coast of Ireland where he founded the monastery of Mayo. Feast day: February 18.

COLUMBA (521–597)

Also known as Columcille, Colm, or Colum, this Irish monk founded the island monastery of Iona, Scotland, where the Book of Kells probably began. His love of learning was legendary, and he spent seventeen years engaged in intense study, teaching and copying manuscripts. He was also a wandering evangelist who established more than twenty monasteries, many of them on islands, such as Skye. A former druid, Columba composed poems, hymns and other works. Feast day: June 9. (See pp. 169–171, 220–222.)

COLUMBAN (543?–615)

Also known as Columbanus, he was renowned for his strict discipline and austerity. But he is best remembered as the foremost Celtic missionary, founding numerous monasteries throughout Europe and helping re-Christianize the continent. He was also an accomplished scholar who wrote poems and monastic rules. Courageous, uncompromising and zealous, Columbanus did more than any other figure to spread the flame of Celtic Christianity throughout the world. Feast day: November 23. (See pp. 198–200.)

CUTHBERT (634?–687)

A bishop of Lindisfarne monastery on Holy Island, England, Cuthbert may have been born in Ireland. Although he would have preferred to live a life of solitude, Cuthbert was an inspired leader. Still, after years of travel, public preaching and administrative work, he retreated to the island of Farne, where he died. Feast day: March 20. (See pp. 159, 218.)

ENDA (?–530?)

Founder of the influential monastery on Inishmore, the largest of the three Aran Islands, Enda is hailed as the father of Irish monasticism. Tradition has it that Enda's was the first Irish monastery, although the claim is difficult to prove. More certain is the profound influence Enda had on numerous disciples who studied with him, including Brendan, Finian of Clonard, and Columba. Monks and visiting students marveled at Enda's strict asceticism. Feast day: March 21. (See p. 132.)

Kevin (?–618)

A humble hermit who went to Glendalough to be alone with God, Kevin soon attracted a following which turned his solitary retreat into one of the biggest and busiest monastic cities in all of Ireland. A mystic with the heart of an artist, he wrote the rule for his community in verse, and also composed music. His beautiful community was a popular pilgrimage destination for centuries, and today it is one of Ireland's most popular tourist sites. Feast day: June 3. (See chapter 7.)

Patrick (390?–461?)

The patron saint of Ireland, Patrick wasn't the first person to preach Christianity in Ireland, but he was the most effective. Raised in a Roman family in England, Patrick was taken to Ireland as a slave by raiders. He escaped, but once he got home he received a vision from God calling him to evangelize the Irish. He devoted himself to his task wholeheartedly, often reinterpreting ancient pagan Celtic traditions and using them to point to the Creator God. His "Confession," which is still in print, was one of the first documents to be written in Ireland. Feast day: March 17. (See chapter 6.)

The following resources contain much more information on these and other Celtic saints:

- *Wisdom of the Celtic Saints* by Edward Sellner does an excellent job of summarizing the lives and the main teachings of many of the most important Celtic saints.
- Sean McMahon's *Rekindling the Faith: How the Irish*

Re-Christianized Europe is a good catalog of key Celtic saints.

- Floris Books in Edinburgh, Scotland, has published small, inexpensive, nicely done biographies of Patrick, Columba, Brigid, and Brendan. These are available from American distributor Dufour Editions in Chester Springs, Pennsylvania. Phone: (610) 458-5005. Dufour also offers John O'Meara's excellent translation of *The Voyage of St. Brendan*.
- Liam de Paor's *Dictionary of Celtic Saints* and his earlier *St. Patrick's World* are excellent resources.
- Adomnan's *Life of St. Columba* is an intriguing original source.
- Finally, Frederick Buechner's novel *Godric* is a stunning look into the life of an ascetic eleventh-century English monk who had much in common with earlier Celtic saints.

A Celebration of Song

Riverdance and *Lord of the Dance* have done more to popularize Celtic music and dance than anything else this century. These two popular dance revues, along with their bestselling soundtracks and videos, have introduced millions to the magic of Celtic culture.

The music of the Celtic people is imbued with a deep, spiritual power which has its roots in their mythology and history.

Dagda, or "Good God," was one of the most powerful Celtic deities. With his harp, "The Oak of the Two Greens," Dagda played three kinds of music: sorrow-strains, laugh-strains, and sleep-strains. Dagda's legend lives on. The harp has long been a symbol of Irish culture, and is featured prominently in the currency and postage stamps of Ireland. Gods like Dagda were believed to be vehicles through which a mythical music called "Oran Mor" or creation's all-embracing melody flowed.

Bards also contributed to the Celts' musical culture. The bards used their gifts for lyrical poetry to hail the rulers and heroes of their day, often singing their verses at the top of their lungs, so they could be heard over the din of noisy banqueters. Usually accompanied by a harp or another instrument, the bards may have been among the world's first folk musicians.

Centuries later, the Christian poet Caedmon received the gift of song from God. A simple man who couldn't sing a note, he fell into a deep sleep, and in a dream he saw a man calling out to him: "Sing about the Creation of all things." Caedmon spontaneously sang verses in praise of God the Creator:

> Praise we the Fashioner now of Heaven's fabric,
> The majesty of his might and his mind's wisdom,
> Work of the world-warden, worker of all wonders,
> How he the Lord of Glory everlasting,
> Wrought first for the race of men Heaven as a rooftree,
> Then made the Middle East to be their mansion.

🔹 Musical miscellany

Today, a cornucopia of Celtic music flows from (or is inspired by) the lands which were once inhabited by the Celts: Ireland, Scotland, Wales, Brittany (France), and Galicia (northwest Spain).

In the early 1950s, the Clancy Brothers began performing traditional Irish music in Greenwich Village coffee houses. Today, Enya is the most omnipresent contemporary Irish artist, selling millions of albums of Celtic-inspired music. The Chieftains, founded in 1963, are traditional Irish music's undisputed ambassadors to the world. They've recorded more than three dozen albums and played thousands of concerts around the globe. The Tannahill Weavers are a Scottish quintet that have done their part to introduce fans in many lands through their collections of Celtic music and song. And James Galway is both a critically acclaimed classical musician and a popular entertainer who has been exploring his cultural roots on solo albums like *Celtic Minstrel* and *Legends*, which was recorded with pianist Phil Coulter.

Most contemporary Celtic music uses guitar, flutes, whistles, fiddles, the bodhran drum, and the uilleann pipes, as well as the accordion, the harmonica, and the hammered dulcimer.

In the rock era, numerous bands have tried to marry the beauty of Celtic music to the aggressiveness of rock, and nobody's done it better than Clannad, the band that Donegal siblings Maire, Pol, and Ciaran Brennan founded in 1970. Their 1998 album, *Landmarks*, their seventeenth, is a good introduction to their haunting, mystical music. And lead singer Maire Brennan's third solo album, *Perfect Time*, is a beautiful exploration of Celtic Christianity.

Contemporary Christian recording artist Jeff Johnson, an Oregon-based Christian composer and keyboardist, has contributed to many Windham Hill Celtic collections, and his *Navigatio* album is a tribute to St. Brendan. Iona, a British band named after Columba's famous monastery, features six instrumental virtuosi who mix progressive rock, jazz fusion, and melodic pop with lyrics about mysticism, the transcendence of God, and the Book of Kells.

You can begin building your collection by contacting three labels which have done the most to give Celtic music the attention it deserves. The simplest way to start your Celtic music collection is to send five dollars to:

Maggie's Music
P.O. Box 4144
Annapolis, MD 21403
Phone (410) 268-3394

In return, Maggie's will send you a compact disc sampler featuring the label's artists. You'll also receive a catalog, which will give you a chance to order the label's regularly priced releases, including four superb Celtic Christmas releases.

Narada is a Milwaukee-based "New Age" label which offers a dozen Celtic releases. *Celtic Odyssey* and *Celtic Legacy* are two highly recommended samplers that include a wide range of artists. If it's difficult to find these in a store near you, call Narada at (414) 961-8350.

In 1996, Green Linnet Records in Danbury, Connecticut, released its *Twentieth Anniversary Collection*, a two-CD set which features thirty-eight selections by various artists. Also worthwhile is the label's 1990 collection, *The Celts Rise Again*. For information, call (203) 730-0333.

If you want to read about Celtic music, pick up *Bringing It All Back Home*, the companion book to the BBC television series, or *Irish Traditional Music*, Ciaran Carson's quirky but interesting book. For all of the latest information, there's *Dirty Linen* magazine, which is available in many stores or by subscription for $20 a year for six issues. For information call (410) 583-7973.

SACRED SITES

Ireland brims over with breathtaking sites that are rich in tradition. Here's an alphabetical listing of ten of the most interesting and rewarding places to visit.

Aran Islands

Inishmore, the largest of the three rugged, rocky Atlantic islands located west of Galway, is a land outside time. Easily accessible via ferry rides from Galway Bay, you can see the island by tour van, but many choose to rent a bike from one of the many dockside rental companies.

The site of Enda's important monastery, which features an old ruin surrounded by numerous graves, is approximately five minutes away from the ferry port by bike. Farther away, but well worth the trip, is Dun Aengus, the impressive ancient stone fort located on a cliff hundreds of feet above the crashing sea. (See p. 32.)

Clonmacnoise

Founded by Ciaran around 549, this was one of Ireland's most important monastic settlements and schools. Located south of present day Athlone at a site that was once a busy crossroads of an ancient overland route and the beautiful River Shannon, Clonmacnoise has many impressive remains, dozens of impressive carved crosses and one of Ireland's best preserved round towers.

A modern tourist center offers an informative audio-visual presentation which gives the history and impact of this once famous monastic center. Also available are tours of the grounds, and many private companies offer boat tours of the Shannon. (See p. 133)

❖ Dublin

One could spend countless days exploring this storied and charming city, but two tours are particularly relevant. Trinity College's Book of Kells display is an awe-inspiring introduction to this masterpiece of Celtic Christian art. And the Literary Pub Crawl, which departs nightly from a local pub, provides a fun and free-wheeling introduction to Ireland's ongoing literary legacy.

❖ Dunbeg Fort

The stunning Dingle Peninsula is the site of this well-preserved stone fort, west of the town of Dingle. Built some 2,500 years ago, this massive fort would have provided solid protection to an extended Celtic clan, and the surrounding ditches and mounds would have exposed attackers to easy ambush. Though part of the fort has fallen into the sea below, this is still one of the best preserved of Ireland's nearly 40,000 forts.

While in the area, you can also examine the impressive stonework of the Gallarus Oratory and an ancient installation of Ogham Stones. (See chapter 2.)

🍀 Glendalough

One can see why St. Kevin established his monastery in this beautiful valley in the Wicklow Mountains.

Hundreds of thousands of people visit this impressive site every year. The tourist center is a bit busy at times, but walk a few minutes on one of the park's many hiking trails, which wind through woods and along a lake, and you'll experience the seclusion Kevin knew.

An hour or two south of Dublin, Glendalough has a classy hotel, comfy bed and breakfasts, good restaurants, and affordable Irish sweaters. (See chapter 7.)

🍀 Hill of Slane

Located near Drogheda, this little-visited historic site marks the spot where St. Patrick made his symbolic stand against the pagan Celts. By lighting a bonfire atop the hill during the important pagan celebration of Beltane, Patrick subverted this ancient ritual and stated his claim that Ireland would be a Christian island.

With cemetery ruins and a tower that offer plenty of opportunities for climbing and photo taking, Slane is off the beaten track but well worth the visit. (See pp. 111–112.)

🍀 Hill of Tara

Located less than an hour northwest of Dublin by car, this fabled spot was the most sacred site in Ireland for centuries. Long the seat of Ireland's High King, the hill was an important setting for civic gatherings and pagan rituals. Excavations are unearthing new discoveries, and the church at the foot of the hill offers an informative audio-visual presentation on the hill's epic past. (See p. 15.)

🔹 Monastic sites

Ireland was once home to hundreds of monastic settlements. Among the most important sites are many which still reward the curious visitor:

- At Monasterboice, near Drogheda, one can still see many of the finely carved Celtic crosses that were produced in the monastery's workshop.
- Near the southern coastal town of Ardmore, St. Declan's monastery features ruins, a large cemetery and an impressive round tower.
- And Kildare, the site of Brigid's famous double monastery, features a well-preserved round tower.

🔹 Newgrange

Easily reached from Dublin, this 5,000-year-old burial monument is Ireland's most incredible ancient site. Built centuries before Stonehenge by a pre-Celtic people that shared the Stonehenge builders' fascination with astronomy, Newgrange is a marvel of engineering and an enduring monument to the belief in the immortality of the soul.

A new visitors' center contains numerous displays and presentations and offers regular tours of the monument and other nearby sites. Newgrange shouldn't be missed by anyone interested in Ireland's ancient heritage. (See chapter 13.)

🌀 Skellig Michael

Not for the armchair traveler, this stunning monastic outpost requires strong legs, and the eight-mile boat ride from Portmagee into the choppy Atlantic is not for those prone to seasickness.

Seldom is a journey worth so much. The monks who established this remote outpost fourteen centuries ago wanted silence and solitude, and they got plenty of both on this steep, rocky, windswept island. The thousands of steps they built rise up from the sea, taking visitors to the painstakingly preserved monks' quarters and a small chapel erected out of carefully constructed stones and not a bit of mortar.

For the more cautious, a visitors' center located on Valentia Island describes the fascinating history of the island. (See chapter 8.)

Acknowledgments
and Resources

I would like to thank Scott Waxman of the Scott Waxman Agency for making this project happen. Scott helped transform my passionate enthusiasm into an actual book.

There are three writers who helped this project more than they will ever know.

Thomas Cahill's eloquent bestseller, *How the Irish Saved Civilization* (Anchor/Doubleday), has introduced many readers to Ireland's amazing monks and scholars.

When I first started doing serious research on Celtic spirituality, I devoured *Wisdom of the Celtic Saints* (Ave Maria Press), a thorough but accessible book by Edward Sellner of the College of St. Catherine in St. Paul, Minnesota; and *The Celtic Monk* (Cistercian Publications), a revealing study of monastic rules by Irish archivist Uinseann O'Maidin of Mount Melleray Abbey in County Waterford. Both gentlemen made many helpful suggestions, and O'Maidin allowed me to use some of the prayers he has collected.

Of the seventy plus books I read or consulted for this project, the following were especially informative and useful: *Ancient Ireland: From Prehistory to the Middle Ages*

(Oxford) is a lavishly illustrated, oversized book and an excellent introduction to nearly 200 major Irish monuments and sites. With stunning photos by Jacqueline O'Brien and an authoritative text by Peter Harbison, the pre-eminent writer in this field, the book makes excellent reading and can help travelers plan an itinerary. Harbison's *Pre-Christian Ireland* (Thames and Hudson) is an acclaimed look at Ireland's prehistoric people.

The following books explore ancient Celtic origins. Nora Chadwick's *The Celts* (Penguin) is an essential history. Anne Ross's *Pagan Celtic Britain* (Academy Chicago Publishers) is dry, but informative. Peter Berresford Ellis's *The Druids* (Eerdmans) is the definitive work on this subject. And two books in the Penguin Classics series provide excellent introductions to important literature: *Early Irish Myths and Sagas* translated by Jeffrey Gantz and Kenneth Hurlstone Jackson's *A Celtic Miscellany*.

John and Caitlin Matthews have translated numerous Celtic texts in more than a dozen books; but they have been criticized for linking little-understood ancient practices to contemporary neo-pagan and New Age activities, a problem that plagues their popular *Encyclopaedia of Celtic Wisdom: A Celtic Shaman's Sourcebook* (Element). More reliable are their *British & Irish Mythology* (Diamond) and *The Celtic Book of Days* (Destiny).

Tracing Celtic history became easier after St. Patrick and others began writing down essential information. Liam de Paor's excellent *St. Patrick's World* (Four Courts Press) is the best study of the early Christian Celts. Lisa Bitel's *Isle of the Saints* (Cork University Press) is a fascinating study of Celtic monasticism. Three brief books about Celtic Christian spirituality provide many helpful insights: John

O'Riordain's *The Music of What Happens* (St. Mary's Press); Philip Sheldrake's *Living Between Worlds* (Cowley); and Michael Mitton's *The Soul of Celtic Spirituality* (Twenty-Third Publications). Bede's *A History of the English Church and People* (Penguin Classics) provides some interesting glimpses of Celtic Christianity, and *Celtic Christian Spirituality: An Anthology of Medieval and Modern Sources* by Oliver Davies and Fiona Bowie (Continuum) is an essential collection of poems, prayers, and prose.

Collections of Celtic prayers constitute a booming cottage industry. Esther deWaal's *The Celtic Way of Prayer* (Doubleday) is one of the best. Bernard Meehan's *The Book of Kells* (Thames and Hudson) is a fascinating, beautifully illustrated look at this important work. And Steve Lawhead's sprawling novel *Byzantium* (Harper/Zondervan) uses Celtic monasteries as a backdrop for a thrilling ride through ancient times.

If you're considering a visit to Ireland, consult these excellent guides: *The Boyne: A Valley of Kings* (by Boylan; published by O'Brien); *The Dublin Literary Pub Crawl* (Costello; Farmar); *A Guide to Britain's Pagan Heritage* (Clarke; Hale); *Music Lover's Guide to Great Britain & Ireland* (Bianchi and Gusoff; Passport); *The Holy Wells of Ireland* (Logan; Colin Smythe); *Glendalough: A Celtic Pilgrimage* (Rodgers and Losack; Morehouse); and *The Skellig Story* (Lavelle; O'Brien).

These American distributors are helpful in locating many of the above titles: Dufour Editions, phone (610) 458-5005; Irish Books and Media (612) 871-3505; and Irish American Book Company (303) 530-1352. If that doesn't work, contact Kenny's Bookshop and Art Gallery in Galway, Ireland (e-mail: queries@kennys.ie).

TALKS AND TOUR

Steve Rabey is available for lectures on the subjects discussed in this book.

Also, in the fall of 1999, Steve and Lois Rabey plan to lead a "Celtic Spirituality" tour of Ireland featuring many of the sites discussed in this book.

For information, fax your request to (719) 488-2479.

Index